LEADING THE

Millennial

CHURCH

How to reach an ever-changing generation with
the never-changing message of the Gospel

Jeremy Tuck

LEADING THE

Millennial

CHURCH

How to reach an ever-changing generation with
the never-changing message of the Gospel

Jeremy Tuck

T&J PUBLISHERS

A SMALL INDEPENDENT PUBLISHER WITH A BIG VOICE

Printed in the United States of America by
T&J Publishers (Atlanta, GA.)
www.TandJPublishers.com

All Bible verses are from the King James Version (KJV), New Living Translation (NLT), New International Version (NIV), God's Word Translation (GWT), and the New American Standard Bible (NASB)

Cover design by Timothy Flemming, Jr. (T&J Publishers)
Book format and layout by Timothy Flemming, Jr. (T&J Publishers)

ISBN: 978-0-9997806-1-9

To contact the author, go to:
www.lftchurch.com
pastortuck@lftchurch.com
Facebook: @jeremytuck
Instagram: @jeremytuck
Twitter: @jeremytuck

ACKNOWLEDGEMENTS

First and foremost, I dedicate this book to my Lord and Savior, Jesus the Christ. Without God, I can do nothing. I owe everything to Him.

I also dedicate this book to my beautiful wife, Akila; and my four sons: Jeremiah, Ayden, Austin and Jaxten. I love you all dearly.

Also, I want to thank my parents Annie Tuck and the late Pastor James Tuck, both of whom mean so much to me.

Lastly, I want to thank my Living Faith Tabernacle church family, my friends, and all of my supporters.

"God has given believers the responsibility of spreading the Gospel to all the world, and we need to use all at our disposal to accomplish this task."—Theodore Epp

TABLE OF CONTENTS

WELCOME TO THE NEW MILLENNIUM

*T*HIS IS A NEW DAY. I'M SURE YOU'VE HEARD THAT PLENTY of times before. I'll admit it can sound like a cliché, but it's not one. This truly is a new day, a different day. Just take a moment and think about the differences caused by the enormous advancements in technology. Think about how these advancements have changed not only our methodologies, but our perspectives. Past generations marveled over the creation of the computer. Older generations perhaps thought they were witnessing the end of the world when they beheld the birth of the television, especially the color television. Of course, in almost every generation there have been individuals keenly watching the advancements in technology with a slant towards Bible prophecy, always on the lookout for what might be deemed the "Mark of the Beast" while thinking they were living in "the last days." But today's generation has been exposed to things their parents, grandparents, and great grandparents could only dream about or imagine. Thoughts today seemingly travel further than the vast reaches of outer space and move faster than the speed of light due to the emergence of the internet. Just post your thoughts on Facebook or Twitter and they will go viral, reaching billions of people at one time in an instant. Long gone are the days of sifting through books in a library or hunting for information. If you want or need to know something, just go to Google. The world now sits at your fingertips. Today's technology is truly mind-blowing. For example, in the medical field, we've gone far beyond merely examining a person using x-rays and CAT Scans; we're now in the age of Nonotechnolgy, interjecting inorganic nanoparticles (nanobots as some people call them) of materials synthesized from metals such as gold or silver that range in size from 1 to 100 nm into people's bodies to target and deliver drugs to defective cells while leaving the healthy cells unharmed. This is a marriage between artificial intelligence and medicine the likes we've never seen before. We also see brain-machine interfaces today where computers, computerized prosthetic limbs, and other computerized technologies are able to be controlled by a user's neural signals. And did I even mention genome editing where we can literally build customized babies like we're in a Build-A-Bear store? Or embryonic stem-cell research where scientists are now merging the DNA from different species together and growing human organs inside of pigs and other animals for the purpose of creating human organs on demand? In the business world, business moves at the speed of light. Most products and services are now rendered digitally, thereby causing wait times to become nearly nonexistent. Today's weaponry is the stuff of science fiction, from invisibility cloaks that bend light around 3D objects to nuclear weapons and bombs that can level entire cities that can be carried in briefcases to weather-based weapons, space-based weapons, and biological weapons that can target traits within specific ethnic groups to the latest advancements by DARPA (The Defense Advanced Research Projects Agency) that involve the combining of man, animal, and machine to produce super soldiers. We now have self-driving cars, intelligent self-assembling robots, cashless societies, transgenics, biometrics, anti-gravity propulsion systems, etc.; even crime has received an upgrade. Today, we have a new category of crime: cyber-crime; cyber-warfare; we have a new type of criminal known as a hacker, an individual who can empty out bank accounts, steal identities, and sell the personal information of customers from major retail stores to the highest bidder all while sitting in their basements in their underwear, not to mention shut down important electrical devices such as smart phones, vehicles, planes, etc., and even perhaps compromise the weapons systems of other nations. And that's just the tip of the iceberg. This truly is a new day. It can be scary. Parts of it can be comforting. Hey, at least we can boast that people are living longer. But on the other side of that same coin, we can also shamefully boast that more people today are on psychiatric medications than ever before. Quite frankly, I'm standing here on the precipice of tomorrow asking the question, "What's next? Travel through wormholes in space? Teleportation? Time travel? *What?*" An even more daunting question would be "How much further can we go before destroying ourselves?"

 With all of the changes and advancements in technology, we've also witnessed the rise of new questions and concerns. Fifty years ago, no one thought about cyber-crime and cyber-warfare. These things didn't exist. Years ago, in the halls of academia, there were no talks or discussions about Bioethics. Years ago, a parent didn't have to grapple with how to address sex with their six year old who has been exposed to pornographic content on the internet—you could barely get Playboy on TV, let alone worry about Playboy and Hustler being on your cell phone or smart watch. Welcome to the new millennium.

MILLENNIALS VS. BABY BOOMERS

The millennial generation is the most widely studied and the largest generation in history. Today, there are over seven billion people on the earth, prompting concerns within the international community regarding global warming and the overconsumption of natural resources. The millennial generation is a huge generation, one that has its challenges and differs greatly from the previous generation, the Baby Boomers.

The millennial generation goes by another nickname: the microwave generation. That's right. Oftentimes, when the older generation talks about Millennials, they liken them to microwaves. What they're saying, in essence, is that this generation wants everything to come quick and easy; we don't like to wait…for anything: for success, for love, and even for God. And to be honest, that is a fair assessment. We want quick success, we want instant hookups (just go online and find your next love interest or date), and we want fast church services (an hour and fifteen minutes at the most).

Living in a society that has grown accustomed to having everything move at the speed of sound, patience has become one of those rare qualities. In some circles, patience is a new curse word; it is a death sentence. If you run a business, oftentimes the success of your business depends on the speed in which you work and are able to produce results. It's not enough to merely produce results today; you have to produce results faster than your competitor. The trophy goes to the fastest. Fast food restaurants have certainly capitalized on this new trend. The fast food industry is one of the largest, most lucrative industries in the world today for one reason alone: people don't have time to wait on a good meal anymore, at least that's what many tell themselves. People would rather sacrifice the quality of their food and run the risk of contracting heart-related diseases due to the consumption of foods that are filled with chemicals designed to enhance their taste and extend their shelf-life rather than wait a few minutes longer for a healthy home-cooked meal. I still have a little Old-School in me. I still believe that if you want something cooked right, it has to be cooked slow. Anything that is rushed in the oven may look good on the outside but still be raw on the inside. I still appreciate those oldies too: Teddy Pendegrass, Luther Vandross, Al Green, and others. They understood one thing: intimacy, like food, needs to be done right, which means sometimes you just need to take… it…slow. Unfortunately, in today's culture, as is reflected in many of the hit songs on the radio, the goal has shifted from building solid relationships on the foundation of trust, honesty, and respect to simply scoring in the bedroom. Maybe I'll talk more about that in another book. But just know that it is true that the millennial generation is the microwave generation; it's one that is used to having things their way when they want them; they're not used to waiting, nor are they accustomed to the regular routine of back-breaking labor like their parents and grandparents, many of whom can tell you about picking cotton for hours under the sweltering heat of the sun and making it off of very little. We still have hard times today, but many have a different set of expectations and a sense of entitlement that their parents and grandparents didn't come up with. This marks a fundamental difference between Millennials and Baby-Boomers. Previous generations were taught life doesn't owe anyone anything and that they had to work for everything they got. Our grandparents learned that if they wanted food, then they had to grow it, kill it, skin it, clean it, then prepare it, cook it, and finally eat it; they couldn't just go to Krogers and find it readily available and even precooked. If they needed clothes, they had to get a needle and some thread and make their own clothes. If they wanted to go to school, they had to walk for several miles in the sun, the rain, and even the snow just to get to school; they couldn't just stand next to their mailboxes and expect a bus to swing by and pick them up. If they wanted rights and privileges, they had to get out and fight for them, not sit back and complain about what they're not being given. They grew up with a different mentality. They came up expecting to fight, struggle, and wait for everything. But not Millennials. Millennials don't hold the same expectations. Many Millennials are under the impression that someone is supposed to hand them what they don't have: Kroger will give them food, the government will give them food-stamps and other assistance, clothing stores will clothe them, law officials will protect them, city officials will clear their streets for them when they're covered in snow, etc. Millennials don't farm. Millennials don't sew. Millennials sometimes act as if they don't know how to get a shovel and remove the snow from their own front yards at times. This generation isn't simply the microwave generation; it is the structurally dependent generation.

In a recent poll conducted by the Barna Research group, "four out of every ten adults say they prefer socialism to capitalism."[1] One Harvard study has found that "46 percent [of young adults between ages 18 and 29] had positive views of capitalism, and 47 percent had negative views" and that in "2011, for example, the Pew Research Center found that people ages 18 to 29 were frustrated with the free-market system."[2] What that means is Millennials think differently from Baby-Boomers in terms of government and the free market. Today, Millennials tend to lean more towards the idea that the government should be our benefactor, providing us with goods and services that are traditionally seen as the responsibility of the citizens. For example, rather than private health care companies providing health insurance at competitive rates to those who can afford to pay, today's Millennials would prefer to see the government provide healthcare to all through a socialized healthcare system. Millennials tend to lean more towards an authoritarian style of government due to their insistence on a system of fairness for all and their disillusionment with American capitalism, which allows for such disparities between the rich and the poor.

The differences between Millennials and Baby-Boomers are often displayed in the job market. For example, one of the biggest gripes that employers and organizations have with Millennials is that they're less stable than their predecessors; this highlights a problem with discipline. Many companies struggle with the problem of being able to keep employees on their jobs for a significant amount of time due to the inability of many Millennials to commit to anything. Baby-Boomers have gained a reputation of being committed in their places of work, committed to their chosen causes, and committed even to organizations such as the church. Companies like AARP are glad to have Baby-Boomers sign-up with them over Millennials, knowing that Baby-Boomers have a tendency to stay committed whereas Millennials struggle with commitment. Some of us have parents and grandparents who boast about working on a single job for forty and fifty years, all the way up until retirement. Today, it's easy to find a millennial who has held ten to twenty different jobs in a single year. I'm aware of certain factors: social factors, economic factors, etc. I'm not talking about someone who was laid off from work due to downsizing. I'm talking about someone who quit ten different jobs in a single year out of boredom and the incessant fear of missing out on something better. We see this trend even in finances and relationships. An article entitled *Marriage And Money: Key Differences Between Millennials And Boomers* states, "[baby] boomers have more financial discipline. When confronted with something they want but can't afford, boomers are more likely to not buy it. Forty-nine percent of boomers accept that they don't have enough money for the purchase, and they move on. But only 37% of Millennials accept that limit." The article goes on to say, "Millennials blame a lot of their money woes on peer pressure. Thirty-four percent of them feel pressure to keep up with friends' spending habits. Only 8% of boomers feel that way. And a lot of Millennials' peer pressure is exerted through social media. Forty-six percent blame social media posts. When asked specifically if sharing images and milestones on social media makes them compare their situation with that of others, 64% of Millennials say yes. Only 29% of boomers feel that way." Many Millennials lack the discipline to save for their financial futures unlike Baby-Boomers, and they tend to want to "keep up with the Jones'" who they see a lot of on social media. Of course, discipline sets us up for better tomorrows at the expense of today's fun. Lacking discipline, on the other hand, sets us up for disaster up the road. The attitude of many Millennials as revealed in this article is actually described in the book of Proverbs 6:6-8, which says,

> "Go to the ant, thou sluggard; consider her ways, and be wise: which having no guide, overseer, or ruler, provideth her meat in the summer, and gathereth her food in the harvest." (KJV)

Actually, I like the God's Word Translation (GWS) better. It reads,

> "Consider the ant, you lazy bum. Watch its ways, and become wise. Although it has no overseer, officer, or ruler, in summertime it stores its food supply. At harvest time it gathers its food."

Of course, this reminds me of the story of the ant and the grasshopper: One summer, there was an ant who was hard at work in the field, planting seeds while his neighbor, the grasshopper, was outside enjoying the summer weather, having fun and playing. The grasshopper would ask the ant, "Mr. Ant, why are you working so hard? Why don't you chill and have fun like me? It's summertime. Enjoy the weather like me." The ant wouldn't say anything; he would simply keep working. Finally, fall came and the ant was still working, this time harvesting his food. The grasshopper was still relaxing and having fun, enjoying the nice weather. But then, winter came. During winter, there was no food available. The grasshopper found himself starving while the ant was nestled safely and comfortably in his home with plenty to eat. Why? Because the ant disciplined himself and saved up during the summer months in preparation for the winter months. It is important that we, as Millennials, take heed to what the Bible tells us here. There will be winter months ahead, and I'm not talking about the weather. It is therefore wise to sacrifice today's fun in order to secure ourselves tomorrow. As the saying goes: "Smile now, cry later. Or cry now, smile later."

Regarding relationships and marriage, my next statement shouldn't shock you: Millennials have a much more difficult time committing themselves to marriage. For example, one Gallup poll revealed that 59% of Millennials fall under the category of "Single/Never Married" while only 10% of Baby-Boomers fall into that category. On the flip-side, 9% of Millennials are currently in living arrangements with domestic partners as opposed to the 3% of Baby-Boomers living in such arrangements.[3]

In that same study, it is stated that "Millennials are clearly delaying marriage longer than any generation before them, in spite of evidence suggesting that many Millennials intend to marry at some point."[4] Millennials don't value marriage as much, but they are more inclined, according to this poll, to have children out of wedlock greatly due to today's increased acceptance of the practice. The article also adds that Millennials "are more than twice as likely as older Americans to identify as LGBT" due to the acceptance of these alternative lifestyles in society today.

TODAY'S CHURCH

The differences between Millennials and Baby-Boomers I just covered are just a few of the differences between the two groups; their are so many more to expound on. But just these few differences alone pose a huge challenge, especially as it pertains to the place of worship, the church. The church has become the new battlefield where different generations with contrasting world-views come face to face. And the big problem is God placed a mandate on both sides to come into agreement, touching and agreeing before He decides to move. This can feel like God tied the tails of a cat and a dog together and then gave the pastor the seemingly impossible task of making both animals get along and walk in unison. Talk about a headache? Because of the differences between these two groups, churches have experienced nasty splits; some pastors, unable to deal with the stress of attempting to reconcile two generations under one roof, have taken off their collars and hung up their robes and quit the ministry altogether. In many churches, rather than both groups working together, either one group has won the culture war within that church or the other group has won, and this has thereby caused that church to alienate a particular demographic. For example, some churches are either entirely young or entirely old; there is no mixture of the young and the old. In many churches, the seasoned saints show up with their knives and the younger saints show up with their hatchets, and caught in the middle of both sides is the lowly pastor who is often torn between sides while trying to get them to agree on what the Bible says is the right way.

Throughout the course of this book, I am going to elaborate on the reasons behind the differences in the way Millennials and Baby-Boomers think and reveal to you strategies from the Word of God on how to reconcile these differences by successfully addressing the needs of each group and showing them how their differences aren't a detriment, but a benefit to the Body of Christ.

CHAPTER ONE

THE ANIMAL KINGDOM

*I*N THE FIELD OF COUNSELING, THERE IS ONE RULE THAT reigns supreme: you must be a good listener. If you talk to any marriage counselor or therapist who deals with family problems, they'll tell you that one of the biggest problems most couples and families have is the inability to communicate properly. Many people yell rather than talk; they shout at each other rather than listening to each other to get an understanding of what they're feeling and why they're feeling the way they do. And sadly, the same scenario plays out on a large scale in the church. Rather than engaging in the art of listening with the intent to hear the other group's perspective, different generations within the sanctuary walls often spend their time throwing cheap shots at one another ("These youngsters can't tell me anything. They don't know about 'real church' and hard times. We need to go back to the old time way." "These old folks are out of touch. They don't know about the world we live in and the things we're facing."). We say things like this for the purpose of exerting dominance over one another and gaining bragging rights in order to prop up our generation as the supreme generation boasting the most brilliant minds. Basically, the very thing that keeps husbands and wives arguing with each other rather than hearing each other out is the same thing that keeps separate generations in church fighting one another rather than working together: ego. One side wants to be right. One side wants to dominate. Neither side realizes that they can accomplish more for God's Kingdom if they work together and listen to one another. One group brings the wisdom while the other brings the energy and innovations needed to evangelize properly in this day and time. One side keeps us grounded by connecting us to our roots while another side prevents us from becoming complacent by connecting us to our tomorrow. Both groups need each other. God placed gifts inside of both groups. But the key to unlocking our full potential as Millennials and Baby-Boomers alike is to drop pride and ego and listen to one another. Believe it or not, both sides have much to teach each other.

EATING THE FUTURE

In the animal kingdom, certain species of animals have been known to cannibalize their own. Female spiders often outsize their male counterparts and will usually kill and eat their male suitors after sex. *I know. Disgusting!* Polar bears and grizzlies have been known to eat smaller bears. Certain types of sharks have been known to eat their own—particularly, the sand tiger shark. With these sharks, they begin their cannibalistic practices while in the womb. The larger embryos will devour their smaller siblings while still in gestation. You

24

can imagine how vicious they are once out of the womb.

There is one practice that has become commonplace in many churches throughout the years: it is the cannibalistic practice of the elder saints devouring the younger saints. In churches where the culture war between different generations is in full swing, we see this a lot: young people are driven out of church because of their differences in approach and methodology as it pertains to evangelism and worship. Millennials want to wear jeans, t-shirts, and turn worship services into mini concerts with all of the latest and greatest in technology in the background. Millennials want Starbucks in the lobby and stage lights in the sanctuary. Older generations tend to shy away from such things. Truthfully, every generation has pushed the envelop further than their predecessors. When Thomas A. Dorsey, the writer of the gospel classic "Precious Lord," first emerged onto the church scene, he was rejected by traditionalists as too worldly to play in churches. Being that he was a musician playing in night clubs, he introduced a new sound into the church. Today, we affectionately refer to Thomas A. Dorsey as the father of gospel music. What was new decades ago has become a tradition today, and it was first despised before being accepted. Anytime something new is introduced into the church there will be individuals who call it worldly and will speak out against it, which tends to be part of the problem. The next generation will always introduce a new way of doing things in the church. The question is can the current and older generations handle it? Can they embrace the fact that the church will not always look like the church they've seen and have grown up in? There will always be a church, but it will not always look like that which we've seen growing up. Is that bad? No, it isn't. As long as the timeless message of the Gospel isn't tampered with, then the change in methodology shouldn't become a source of contention in the church.

Older generations have always benefited from the advancements made by younger generations. For example, grandma would tell you that she prefers to have a modern washer and dryer as opposed to washing clothes in a tub of hot water and hanging them on clothes lines outside to dry. Grandma has a smart phone too, and she knows how to work it; she will text you, surf the web, use the navigational device, and more. The older generation doesn't ride to church in horse-and-buggies; they pull up in church parking lots in style, riding clean in their Cadillacs, Mercedes, Toyotas, Hondas, Nissans, BMW's, etc. Some of them even have the nerve to swerve into the parking lot with a gangsta' lean and park in the Chairman of the Deacon Board's parking spot where everyone can see them; some will have the audacity to glance at their Apple watches during service just to show them off and to indicate to the preacher that they are preaching a little too long. Reports have revealed that people today are living longer due to the advancements made in medical science. New technologies allow doctors to detect and diagnose problems they once couldn't detect using older machines. I threw these examples out to stress a point, which is this: When it comes to society, the older generations are eager to rock the latest technological gadgets, all of which offer more convenience and comfort in their lives, but when it comes to church, they tend to shun the latest approaches to worship and evangelism and cling onto to the old ways of doing things. This is a double-standard because those who're steadily screaming that they want to go back to "the old time way" in church do not—and I repeat, "DO NOT!!!"—want to return to the horse-and-buggy, dial up telephones, archaic medical technologies, clunk-box television sets with the grainy images, slow and less effective household appliances, etc. Why, then, do they insist on the worship experience not receiving an upgrade? The reason for this is also the cause behind their cannibalization of the younger generation of saints. What is the reason? Well, I'll tell you in one word: fear. It is the fear of becoming irrelevant. No one wants to be forgotten and shut out into the cold while the rest of the world marches on like a marching band in a parade. No one! And yet, the irony is, the youth will march forward like a marching band without the elder saints out of resentment towards them for trying to hold them back due to fear. Fear actually produces the very things we fear the most. Young people with church hurt in their hearts will start churches, but will shun the involvement of their predecessors out of resentment. This is the same thing with women in the church: they will start their own ministries and churches, but they'll keep unto themselves out of anger towards those pastors who shun women in the pulpit. This leads to the fragmentation of the church, creating cliques. This causes the body to become disjointed. And if there is one thing we don't need today, especially in the face of Satan's well structured, well oiled kingdom, which is running the world today and firing on all cylinders (ruling the media, Hollywood, academia, politics, etc.), is a disjointed, confused, fragmented church filled with cannibalistic saints seeking to eat each other out of a desire for supremacy and out of the fear of becoming irrelevant.

Satan trains his servants to pass the torch for the purpose of keeping his agenda going. Do we as Christians do the same?

Jesus knew that His time on the earth was short. He didn't try to change the world in thirty plus years. Instead, Jesus took a different approach: He recruited twelve men and imparted into them the principles of the Kingdom of God and gave them authority and the Holy Spirit and empowered them to finish the work He began. It would have been silly of Jesus to step in every time the disciples were faced with a demon-possessed person and steal their moment. In the Luke chapter ten, we find Jesus sending His disciples (over seventy of them) out in pairs and commissioning them to preach the Kingdom of God to the Jews while healing the sick and casting out demons in His name. Jesus made them do the work. He showed them first, then let them loose so that they could get experience under their belts, get their hands dirty, get a taste and feel for what it means to walk in the very power that Christ walked in. In essence, what Jesus was doing to His disciples was prepping them to take the torch and carry the work of the Kingdom forward after He left. Passing the torch is important. In order to have this mentality, one must be more committed to a cause than they are to themselves; they must see the big picture and realize that the overall cause is more important than their own mortality, ego, and sense of self-worth. This is the true definition of humility. As C.S. Lewis said, "Humility is not thinking less of yourself; it is thinking of yourself less." Thinking of the future helps us to realize the need to prepare today. Thinking of the overall picture—the fact that there is a dying world out there filled with people who're on their way to a burning hell—helps us to put our egos aside and do whatever it takes to get the Gospel message out to the lost. This is one of the things that propelled Paul Crouch, Sr. to start Trinity Broadcasting Television (TBN). Paul Crouch's parents who were devout Christians believed that television was satanic and worldly and they shunned it; so, what a surprise when their own son, Paul, received the unction from God to start a...television ministry. When thinking about it, it is greatly due to TBN that the Gospel is reaching countries and remote locations all over the globe today at an alarming rate. Paul had to get beyond what was a cultural belief that he had been brought up with and see the bigger picture: that God wanted to use the medium of television as a tool to spread the Gospel. You must get beyond yourself and plug into what God is trying to do today. You must forget about your convenience and be moved by a sense of urgency to reach the lost...by any means necessary.

Jesus, in all of His efforts to impart wisdom and humility into His disciples and get them on one accord to promote the Kingdom of God, still faced the problem of egotism in His disciples. Several times we see division among the disciples. One example is found in Luke 10:44-46, which says,

"Let these sayings sink down into your ears: for the Son of man shall be delivered into the hands of men. But they understood not this saying, and it was hid from them, that they perceived it not: and they feared to ask him of that saying. Then there arose a reasoning among them, which of them should be greatest." (KJV)

While Jesus was speaking to His disciples about His up-coming crucifixion and the need to prepare themselves to take the work of evangelism forward, the disciples were concerned with themselves, with who would be the greatest; it was all about the ego with them. They began fighting with each other over status. The fight over status is what's eating many churches up today, destroying them from within. Status is all about position and prestige, being seen and acknowledged, having dominion over others and being looked up to by others. And yet, Jesus counteracted this attitude in the following verses:

> "But Jesus, knowing what they were thinking in their heart, took a child and stood him by His side, and said to them, 'Whoever receives this child in My name receives Me, and whoever receives Me receives Him who sent Me; for the one who is least among all of you, this is the one who is great.'" (vs. 47-48, KJV)

Jesus mentioned that "the least" is the greatest in God's eyes—by "the least," He was referring to the one who serves others rather than seeking to be served by others. The servant is the one who isn't thinking of him or herself; they're thinking about the needs of others more than their own needs. Servants focus on the work, not their images and their statuses. True servants don't even seek to receive special recognition for doing what they are expected to do. Jesus said in Luke 17:9-10, "Will he thank the servant because he did what he was told to do? So you also, when you have done everything you were told to do, should say, 'We are unworthy servants; we have only done our duty'" (NIV). Anytime our desire is to be seen and praised by men for what we do, then God no longer considers us to be servants, and hence, He no longer considers us to be great in His eyes; we actually begin to lose favor with God. We lose our status with God when we seek to gain status with men. God promises to elevate us as long as we are not seeking to elevate ourselves.

The work of ministry is too big for one person; in fact, it's too big for one generation. Satan never sleeps nor slumbers, and neither does God. Satan is always turning up the heat on his program; hence, where "sin abounded, grace did much more abound" (Romans 5:20). God not only matches Satan's intensity; He surpasses it. It is not God's will that His church lag behind the enemy in innovation, technology, finances, and ingenuity. The church is not designed to keep up with the world; it is designed to lead the world. God anointed the Nation of Israel to succeed and prosper; and hence, most of the world's leading technologies and innovations come out of Israel. But we've forgotten that, as the Apostle Paul mentioned in Romans chapter eleven, God blessed the gentile Believes in order to make the Jews jealous. What that means is God has anointed His church to succeed and prosper even more and to take the lead in the marketplace, in the engineering field, in the sciences, the arts, entertainment, technology, etc. We have the anointing, we have the greatest mentor in the universe (the Holy Spirit), why then are we suffering with defeat and are trailing behind the world in just about every area? Why do the most creative

31

minds flock to the world, feeling as if they have no place in the church? Why do the most creative musicians and artists turn to the world to make a living, feeling as if they can't make a living singing in the church? It's simple: Rather than embrace methodological change, we fight it; we cannibalize our future while boasting about our past. In the meantime, souls are busting hell wide open.

JESUS' PRAYER

Jesus revealed in one of His prayers what He foresaw as the biggest threat and hindrance to the success of the church in His day and in ours. The prayer we deem "The Lord's Prayer" is not really the Lord's prayer; it is the prayer Jesus taught us to pray (it should be deemed "Our Model Prayer"). The real "Lord's Prayer" is found in the Gospel of John chapter seventeen. There, Jesus prayed for the church. Jesus' main concern for the church as revealed in His prayer is that we'd be unified rather than divided. Jesus prayed,

"I ask on their behalf; I do not ask on behalf of the world, but of those whom You have given Me; for they are Yours; and all things that are Mine are Yours, and Yours are Mine; and I have been glorified in them. I am no longer in the world; and yet they themselves are in the world, and I come to You. Holy Father, keep them in Your name, the name which You have given Me, that they may be one even as We are." (NASB)

Who needs the devil when we have our own pride and egos as our main enemies? Allowing division to come into the church because of our egos and pride is what Jesus perceived as our biggest threat. He sensed it in His disciples, and He knew it would linger throughout the ages. Our longing for honor would surpass our wisdom and our longing to see God's Kingdom advance in the earth. We would become the type of servants that want to be thanked and even praised for our contributions to the advancement of God's Kingdom in the earth. If the young people don't praise us, then our feelings will be hurt and we'll seek to oppose them. But our work is supposed to be "as unto the Lord" and not unto men for their acknowledgment and appreciation, knowing that God will reward us for the work we've done according to Colossians 3:23-24. When we serve in the ministry for the purpose of being seen, we're no longer servants and we're no longer in line for God's reward; we disqualify ourselves from being rewarded by God. It's only our egos, our desire for praise, recognition, admiration, power, and respect that causes us to cannibalize those who dare to step into our positions and carry the torch forward. Some of us don't mind relinquishing some power to those coming behind us as long as they do things the way we have done things traditionally. We want to mold the future in our image. But God doesn't want carbon copies and clones; He wants originals. God was and is doing a new thing. He loves newness. God creates all things new (Isaiah 43:18-19). When we get born again, we become new (Romans 12:2; Ephesians 4:23). We have a new spirit, a new mentality, a new destiny. In fact, God is getting ready to give the world a makeover (a new heaven and a new earth according to Revelation 21:5). Even God likes to hear a new song (Psalm 96:1). So get ready for the new! It's coming! It's here! Lean into it. Embrace it. Lend it your guidance. Don't try to block it nor reshape it; instead, temper it with your wisdom. Teach the new generation how to weather the storms of life and of ministry rather than criticize them for trying to reach their generation with the Gospel message in a way that's relevant. Put the mission before yourself. Let the sense of urgency to prevent souls from falling into the pits of hell rest on the forefront of your mind.

CHAPTER TWO

WHY THEY DO WHAT THEY DO

HE MOST PROLIFIC UTTERANCE OF CHRIST ON THE CROSS was "Father, forgive them for they know not what they do" (Luke 23:34, KVJ). This highlights one thing: God doesn't merely observe our behaviors; He observes the causes behind our behaviors. Every effect has a cause. Every behavior has a reason behind it. Understanding this helps us to release bitterness, grudges, and resentment, and reconcile broken relationships. Likewise, if Millennials and Baby-Boomers are going to work together, they must first seek to understand each other and discover why they do what they do.

THE RADICAL BABY-BOOMERS

This is the generation of people who were born roughly between 1946 and 1964. This generation came up during a time of great social activism—people were protesting social injustices, war, and poverty. They witnessed the assassinations of a US President (John F. Kennedy) and one of the greatest civil rights leaders in history, Dr. Martin Luther King, Jr. They are the post-war babies whose parents and grandparents experienced two world wars and witnessed firsthand the horrors of the Great Depression. As a result of the things the Baby-Boomers witnessed, they developed a revolutionary, anti-establishment attitude, one steeped in a distrust of the government and of authority figures; hence, they transformed into the hippies and the Civil Rights activists of the 1960's. They defied their parents and rebelled against societal authorities. They frowned on the hypocrisy of those before them who touted themselves as good Christian men and women but were steadily engaging in discriminatory practices against minorities and even performing lynchings and other atrocities *in God's name*. Baby-Boomers in the Black community saw their parents pray for a change while languishing in docility; therefore, they adopted the belief that they needed to do more than just remain on their knees. Many Baby-Boomers began to perceive prayer as a cop-out for some, as a way to remain non-confrontational in order to avoid incurring the wrath of their oppressors. Dr. King, Jr. was perceived as a rebel by his parents and by those who sat at the top of the social power structure (i.e. the government) because he was confrontational. Rather than just "pray about *it*," Dr. King, Jr. spoke about *it*, shouted *it* from the rooftop, marched because of *it*, led boycotts because of *it*, protested *it*, etc. Yes, he was a rebel. He and his peers refused to be passive and docile and simply hope for a change; they demanded it and fought for it. This is the generation who kicked the door of traditional values down, even the positive ones; they proudly smoked pot and engaged in open sex in public places, pursued after non-traditional religious views, sought to be non-conformists at every turn; they wore Afros and dashikis, pumped their black fists in the air, and sung aloud "I'm Black and I'm proud" and "The revolution will not be televised." It was all about attitude, revolution, and change; it was about freeing oneself and becoming independent.

As has been noted by many social scientists, every generation pays attention to the mistakes and problems of the previous generation and seeks to correct those mistakes. In the case of the Baby-Boomers, this is certainly the case. Baby-Boomers' gripe with the ills of their parents' generation caused them to strive even harder to reverse the trends that ruled their parents' generation. For example, their parents, the Traditionalists (those born between 1900–1945), carried certain core values that the Baby-Boomers came to despise. Traditionalists were conformists, putting the collective whole before themselves; and being that they were raised by parents who came straight out of the Great Depression and didn't usually receive the opportunity to go to school, Traditionalists prioritized hard work over education and maintained a strict moral conduct that guaranteed their acceptance in society. With Traditionalists, social acceptance came before personal happiness. People worked to maintain an appearance that earned them acceptance socially. This endeavor created conditions of great misery behind the scenes in many households. For example, it was non-traditional and somewhat unacceptable for wives to work outside of the home; these women were forbidden to step out and explore their dreams; they were relegated to just being homemakers who took care of the house and the kids. And since premarital sex and children born out of wedlock were taboos—and not to mention alternative sexual lifestyles—people generally married not for love, but for convenience, social acceptance, and financial stability. What was missing in many of these homes was happiness and personal fulfillment. The Baby-Boomers sought to uproot many of these traditions, which they viewed as restricting, suffocating, anti-progressive, and oppressive. Baby-Boomers, witnessing the misery in homes due to husbands and wives sacrificing personal happiness on the altar of public acceptance, decided that they would become the first generation to prioritize personal happiness over social acceptance; hence, the baby-boomer generation boasts the highest divorce rate in US history. Their mantra became "My happiness comes first." They officially became the "Me first" generation. Female Baby-Boomers, like other groups in this generation whose parents had been denied or deprived of the opportunity to advance themselves and pursue their dreams, began to view education as a birthright and a doorway to personal fulfillment; they saw personal happiness as an entitlement, not a privilege unlike their parents. As a result of this personal liberation trend, Traditionalists began to refer to Baby-Boomers as perhaps the most greedy and materialistic generation in US history. But Baby-Boomers weren't necessarily selfish, they were just determined not to experience the miseries of their parents; they were focused on getting the most out of life; so they became the most educated generation in US history before the Millennials came; they became anti-establishment, non-conformists who loathed heavy social, moral, and religious impositions that hindered their ability to experience personal happiness and gratification. Baby-Boomers are the ones that adopted the adage "Question everything!" This generation wanted to right the wrongs of their parents, and there were plenty of wrongs to right.

In their pursuit of personal fulfillment (a concept that was embodied in the idea of the American Dream), Baby-Boomers became workaholics, spending fifty to sixty hours or more in the workplace at the expense of quality family time. Like their parents, they were hard workers; but unlike their parents, they worked to advance themselves personally, not advance the company. Every hour spent at the job brought them that much closer to the American Dream, which always seemed just beyond their fingertips. The workplace soon became a source of identity for Baby-Boomers. Baby-Boomers clung to status and the idea of climbing the corporate ladder in order to increase the likelihood of experiencing the American Dream.

One of the main keys to promotion in the workplace—aside from getting results—was being prompt and on time and being visible; you had to be a superstar on the job. But, oh, how things have changed. If you were to talk to a baby-boomer today and ask their advice on success, they'd say you have to work harder; a millennial, on the other hand, would say, "No, you must work smarter." Baby-Boomers accuse Millennials of being spoiled and lazy while Millennials accuse Baby-Boomers of being delusional dinosaurs who are out of touch with society. Such a difference in perspectives breeds contempt between the two generations. Sadly, both generations are running after the same goals while fighting each other because they don't approve of the methods used. Sadly, both generations are alike in so many ways—so many. Baby-Boomers were considered too radical for their parents just as Millennials are now considered too radical to them. I guess it's true what one historian said:

> "The most radical revolutionary will become a conservative the day after the revolution."—Hannah Arendt (1906–1975)

MODERN DAY RADICALS

Millennials are no strangers to war. This is the age of the War of Terror. This is the age of school shootings, church shootings, and terrorist attacks. With all of our surveillance capabilities and technologies, there is an atmosphere of fear similar to that of the Cold War era. Everyone is living on edge, conscious of the fact that weapons have become both deadlier and more concealable.

Millennials are no strangers to social injustices and social conflicts. This generation spends a great deal of time immersing itself in social activism: Occupy Wall Street; Jena Six; marches and protests over police shootings; Black Lives Matter; protesters who kneel during the singing of the US national anthem and the Pledge of Allegiance; women who march on Washington to protest the presidential election while breathing new life into the Feminist Movement; etc. Today, the nation is perhaps more divided than ever, rivaling that of the atmosphere that existed during the Civil War era. Seemingly, every year, there is some major riot or protest in America's streets that takes center stage in the news.

CHPT 2: WHY THEY DO WHAT THEY DO

Millennials are no strangers to hard times and economic downturns. Sure, this generation didn't experience the Great Depression, but they did experience the Great Recession of 2008 where millions of Americans lost their homes, livelihoods, jobs, life's savings, retirements, and material possessions; and in the midst of this rising trend of lost, Millennials experienced the phenomenon of climbing college tuition and the rising cost of living, making Millennials the most indebted generation of all times.

When looking at the situation, Millennials and Baby-Boomers experienced many of the same things; the only difference between the two generations being the emergence of modern technology: Baby-Boomers didn't have Facebook, Instagram, Twitter, and smart phones. Baby-Boomers acquired computers and technology whereas Millennials were born in it and raised in it; it is an integral part of a Millennial's life, unlike Baby-Boomers who see technology as only an accessory. The Millennial generation has never learned how to live without computers, and technology is only getting more advanced as the days go by, making things that were once unobtainable obtainable, things a lot more convenient and accessible, and connecting the world at a rapid pace.

What has technology done to mankind? It has united us like never before. The Millennial generation is the most connected generation since the time of Nimrod. Today, you can have a conversation with someone in Indonesia while sitting in your living room in Nebraska thanks to the internet. This also means Millennials are crossing cultural and national borders and becoming exposed to cultural beliefs and perspectives their parents weren't exposed to. Baby-Boomers set the new political correctness, moral relativism, and sexual revolution trends in motion in America; they not only questioned the moral codes of their parents, but they sought to cast off the restraints of traditional Judeo-Christian morals and create their own moral and ethical codes. We saw an explosion of rebellious, sensual, and anti-establishment behavior in the 1950s, 1960s, and 1970s; we also saw the emergence of non-biblical beliefs and practices during this time period. We can thank the Beatles for exposing the western world to the craze that is known as Eastern Mysticism (the religious beliefs and practices of the eastern world: Yoga, transcendental meditation, eastern philosophical beliefs embedded in many of their religions such as reincarnation, nirvana, karma, etc.); this was when they declared that they had discovered something far more powerful than LSD—they were speaking of transcendental meditation and Yoga and how these two practices can alter one's mental state more than drugs. Today's Millennials have taken it further. Now, elementary school kids throughout America are being made to practice Yoga during Physical Education period in school—they are not running around on the playground playing tag anymore; instead, they're sitting on mats in the gym in the lotus position, conjuring up the Kundalini. Middle schoolers today are made to study and to recite the Five Pillars of Islam in Social Studies classes across the nation. Today, there is very little mention of traditional Judeo-Christian values in schools; the majority of what is taught are beliefs from other cultures outside of the US.

This generation, because of its interconnectedness due to the internet, now carries a more global perspective;

they're not the nationalistic, patriotic type like the previous generations; they're more multi-cultural, being exposed to the lifestyles and belief systems of various cultures from around the world. Today, everything gets exposed. Even countries where there's a dictatorship that tries to suppress their intolerant and oppressive practices and policies, even their dirty laundry gets aired on the world's stage—a photo or a video is bound to leak out onto the internet and go viral. The global paradigm Millennials carry in the US causes them to see America in relation to the international community, which pushes them to seek to dissolve national borders and rid themselves of a national identity.

A Baby-Boomer will most likely have a Bible whereas a Millennial will have a Bible, a Qu'ran, a book on Egyptology, a copy of the Hindu Vedas, Wiccan literature, etc. This is because Millennials thrive on diversity of ideas and multiculturalism. Actually, Millennials are more prone to identify as "Spiritual" rather than religious and boast no affiliation with any single religious institution; they see taking a side as a form of narrow-mindedness; and if there is one cardinal sin in the age of information, it is narrow-mindedness. Millennials, like Baby-Boomers, want to reshape the world and make it a better place, but they tend to lack the spiritual base that Baby-Boomers have; and hence, they take the liberty of pulling from other cultures to re-imagine and reshape America. Moral relativism is the new norm. The fear that Millennials have of back-tracking into the cultural restrictions of yesterday propels them to keep moving forward, innovating, and evolving in thought as well as in machinery. Just like a person who has graduated from a microwave to a modern day highly advance Power Air Fryer or from a flip phone to an advanced Android or iPhone, many Millennials see going back to a strict Bible-belt mentality as de-evolution.

Baby-Boomers often accuse Millennials of being unstable, but in reality, it's just that Millennials have been bombarded with so much information, so many perspectives, ideas, beliefs, and philosophies they've developed a fear of commitment. To Millennials, *stability* is synonymous with *passivity*; it is code-word for "settling for less." Millennials are forever plagued by the prospect of a bigger, better deal. The abundance of options has only intensified the curiosity within them; it has generated within them a fear of "missing out" on something greater; and while all of this is occurring within them, the convenience of the internet has created within them a desire to spend less time in the office and more time finishing projects from their laptops while enjoying their lattes and donuts and meeting new people from the comfort of their local Starbucks. Millennials don't subscribe to the old adage of "Work harder. Be visible and on time." Today, much of the work that gets done is done online; much of the communication is done online; so, for Millennials, it's easier to just focus on the project than the company. Millennials don't feel the need to remain stationary, being that the bulk of their work and their lives exists in the palms of their hands...literally. Millennials aren't lazy or even addicted to their smart phones and laptops; it's just that the marriage of business, technology, and communication has made their laptops and smart phones essential for their survival and an integral part of their lives. Now days, there's no need to drive to the bank to deposit your check—just text a picture of it to the bank through an app on your smart phone from the comfort of your home. That's where technology has taken us all. Cash is becoming obsolete. Offices are becoming obsolete—most goods and services are being rendered digitally. The need to travel is becoming less. Even churches have cyber services where people can tune-in via Facebook Live or live on YouTube and submit their tithes and offerings online through PayPal. *Why go anywhere...unless you really have to?* That is the question asked by Millennials.

Millennials are considered to be narcissistic when, in reality, technology has simply catered to their individualism, giving them a greater opportunity to showcase themselves to the world. Technology didn't create a monster; it just uncaged a monster; it has taken the "Me" attitude popularized by Baby-Boomers and given it a greater platform. Imagine if Baby-Boomers during the Civil Rights and Hippie Movements had Facebook and Twitter. Imagine how many more people Dr. King, Jr. would have reached if he was able to broadcast his messages over Facebook Live. How much more of an impact would he have made? Technology didn't create the cultural and moral revolution we see today; it simply exasperates what already exists in society; it simply amplifies the voices that are ringing aloud; it uncovers the things that have always existed inside of society and inside of the hearts and minds of people, bringing to light the impulses, tastes, desires, and fantasies that have lied buried in every generation. Technology is the great enabler. Traditionalists would have loved to pursue personal fulfillment but they were too afraid to. Baby-Boomers began to pursue personal fulfillment, although limited in many ways. Millennials are able to pursue their dreams because technology has opened up the door to greater possibilities and opportunities.

IT'S ABOUT TRUST

One of the problems Millennials have with the church is a lack of trust. If you were to talk to Millennials today about the church, many of them will admit that one of the issues they're having with church is the lack of transparency and honesty among its leaders and an ever growing skepticism towards the church due to the increase of negative publicity. An article by the Pew Research Center says,

> "Younger generations tend to have more-positive views than their elders of a number of institutions that play a big part in American society. But for some institutions – such as churches and the news media – Millennials' opinions have become markedly more negative in the past five years."[1]

The article goes on to say,

> "Since 2010, Millennials' rating of churches and other religious organizations has dipped 18 percentage points: 55% now say churches have a positive impact on the country compared with five years ago, when nearly three-quarters (73%) said this."

The Barna Research Group also reported,

> "The only piece of information a sizable majority of

Millennials is comfortable sharing with a church is their first name (82%). Only half are willing to give their last names (53%). Just one-third are comfortable sharing their email address (33%). That means two out of three young-adult visitors do not want churches to have that information. Only one in five Millennials are comfortable handing over their physical address (19%), and even fewer their phone number (12%). A mere 6% are willing to grant access on social media, such as friending on Facebook or following on Twitter or Instagram. About one in six Millennials would rather not share anything (15%). Among non-Christian young adults, it's more than one in four (28%)."[2]

Christian evangelist, author, and television personality, John Ankerberg, in his article *Church, Millennials Don't Trust You*, stated several reasons for the growing distrust towards the church by Millennials. Here are two of the reasons he listed as the cause:

"The source of broken trust among Millennials is likely from multiple sources. First, American Millennials are less likely to regularly attend church than previous generations (The Barna Group article notes fewer than half of Millennials have attended church in the past six months.). In short, if a person does not know you, he or she is very unlikely to trust you.

Second, the church's negative publicity continues to increase. From pastoral immorality, to church financial mismanagement, headlines of clergy abuse, and an overall judgmental view of the average church, it's no wonder younger Americans fear sharing personal information with a new church. It is not only a trust issue, but also a safety issue."[3]

Basically, aside from the fact that Millennials are more tolerant of diversity, are much more multicultural, and are therefore prone to view all religions as being equal, which also makes them less likely to commit to the church and attend church services regularly, the increase in negative publicity regarding the church has hammered their trust in the church. In this age of mass exposure, many of the church's dark secrets have been put on blast and the church's credibility in the eyes of Millennials has sustained a critical blow.

In 2016, a famous website named AshleyMadison. com got hacked and all of its members got exposed publicly. Ashley Madison was a subscription based website that provided anonymous sexual hookups to married people looking to engage in infidelity. When the names of the members (mostly men) were leaked out, the public was flabbergasted to find that many of society's outstanding citizens were members of this site. Some of the names on that list belonged to political leaders, judges, policemen, and other public servants; most importantly, among the list of names were the names of many well-known pastors. Many of these individuals were people of impeccable character; now, they were exposed as hypocrites and charlatans, and their credibility was lost. Due to incidents like these, the suspicion and skepticism of Millennials has been heighten, further fueling their desire to search for rings around every collar and the dirt beneath every rug. Public indecency and corruption has always existed in society, but never before has so much of it been publicly exposed. Today, people are finding it difficult—nearly impossible—to keep secret activities secret. Congressmen are getting busted sexting (slang for sending sexually explicit text messages to others) underage girls, nude photos of politicians are going viral (meaning they're being viewed by large numbers of viewers online), secret conversations between leaders are being leaked out into the public, celebrity personalities are getting busted practicing infidelity, radio personalities are being exposed as sexual predators, even the mainstream media is getting caught red-handed in their lies. All of this is fueling great degrees of distrust in Millennials towards those who call themselves public servants and servants of the Most High God.

It is important that we reach and connect with the millennial generation; after all, they are the future of the world, and more importantly, the future of the church. If we fail to reach the millennial generation for Christ, then the church will ultimately fail to carry out its mission in the earth given to it by Jesus the Christ, which is to evangelize the world with the Gospel. If churches don't connect with Millennials, then Satan will. We already see a decline in church attendance by Millennials. We already see a decline in trust towards the church by Millennials. We already see a waive of demonic deception in the form of heretical doctrines being pumped into the minds of Millennials, making them think that Christianity is compatible with every other world religion. In essence, it is obvious that the church is currently losing the culture war and the war for the minds of the next generation. This trend must change. But in order for this trend to begin to change, the church must learn to be transparent, must be integral, must realize that it can no longer hide dark secrets and sweep secret sins under the rug because the watchful eye of technology is always upon it, and it can no longer ignore the tough questions and the most pressing issues of the day. For example, in a hyper-sexualized society, it is absurd that churches treat the subject of sex as taboo while society shapes Millennials' perspectives on the subject through the media. The church must become relevant by addressing the issues and by getting with the times while not abandoning the timeless, immutable message of the Gospel. Yes, you heard me: I said the church must realize that it does no good to hide secret sins and avoid sensitive topics, and that it must become transparent if it is going to regain the trust of Millennials.

In 2007, Senator Chuck Grassley announced his formal investigation into the finances of many church leaders. Among the names of the ministers he was investigating were Creflo Dollar, Benny Hinn, Joyce Meyers, Eddie Long, Paula White, and Kenneth Copeland. Senator Grassley was looking to make a name for himself by unveiling what he considered to be abuses by clergymen looking to get rich. Of course, it also would have benefited the senator to pick up a Bible and read what it says about the principles of seed offerings and tithes. (That's another story.) But the senator's investigation didn't yield the results he had hoped for. There was no foul play among these ministries. Yes, these ministers benefited financially, but as the Apostle Paul mentioned in 1 Timothy 5:18, "the workman is worthy of his wages," and in verse 17 of that chapter, he said elders who preach and teach effectively are worthy of "double honor." Stating their constitutional rights, some of these ministers outright refused to hand over their financial statements to the senator for scrutiny; however, several of them did so gladly, knowing that anything that can improve the church's image in today's culture is a plus—and letting the world see church leaders handling ministry finances with integrity is certainly a huge plus. Joyce Meyers and Benny Hinn among others revealed through transparency that they were not stealing ministry money, and mishandling and wastefully spending ministry finances. This did much to improve the image of the church in the eyes of many, although there is still much work to be done. I can't say the same for Washington, though, as reports of wasteful spending of taxpayer dollars by senators and congressmen is constantly in the news today. Perhaps, Senator Grassley should have been looking in his own backyard for corruption and abuse if he was looking to make a name for himself. But that, too, is another story.

CHAPTER THREE

HOW MUCH IS TOO MUCH?

WAS ONCE ASKED BY SOMEONE, "IF THE opportunity came along and you were asked to be on a reality TV show and allow a cameraman to follow you all around your house, your church, and everywhere else for several months, would you do it?" I'm not going to lie to you: I did give that question some serious thought. The first thought that ran through my mind was *I could certainly use the money that would most likely be offered by the show's producers, and even benefit in certain ways from the exposure*; but then, I began to think about the negative aspects of it. While, on the one hand, it's great to receive exposure for many good things we do, it's not very wise to expose everything to the public that occurs in our everyday lives. It's not necessary that the public sees you and your spouse arguing, you and your kids having communication issues, you having fights with in-laws, you in your pajamas walking around your kitchen, living room, den, etc. Some stuff is not really beneficial to you nor those who're watching. Some stuff, quite frankly, is nobody's business but yours.

There is a misconception many people have today, which is this: total transparency is necessary in order to build trust. That's not true. Some transparency? Yes. Some things we need to reveal to others. But some things we shouldn't reveal. Imagine, if you will, that there was a reality TV show about the President of the United States of America entitled "Meet the First Family" or there was a show entitled "The Real Housewives of Congress"; what if the show's producers were in the room while the President of the United States of America was discussing private plans to topple a dictator in a foreign country, or he or she and their cabinet members were discussing confidential information such as the protocol for a nuclear attack? Some information, if exposed on national television, would harm the nation, not help it. The same goes for the church. Some things shouldn't be discussed in front of a television audience.

Another example of information that shouldn't be shared with the public—or at least, shared with a person or a people who aren't prepared for it—comes from the Bible. In John 16:12, Jesus shared these words: "There is so much more I want to tell you, but you can't bear it now" (NLT). Notice that Jesus sensed the importance of the timing of disclosing certain information. He didn't share information with even His own disciples, sensing that they weren't in a place where they were mentally capable of handling it. Why? They weren't mature enough to handle what He wanted to share with them. In the same sense, some Believers take things to the extreme and divulge information about themselves— personal information—that the public isn't ready (or mature enough) to handle and receive. This misplaced timing results in the untimely death of the sinner's or the baby Believer's faith. The Apostle Peter echoed the same sentiments. He explained that seasoned Believers should not expose certain aspects of themselves to new Believers who aren't ready to handle it; for, in doing so, we can damage a new Believer's faith. Peter wrote, "As free, and not using your liberty for a cloak of maliciousness, but as the servants of God" (1 Peter 2:16). The Apostle Paul also tells us in Romans chapter fourteen to do the same thing. In that chapter, Paul explains to us that the seasoned Believers shouldn't eat and drink things in the presences of new Believers that would cause them to stumble. One good example of this is drinking alcohol. In essence, Paul was explaining to seasoned Believers that they shouldn't drink liquor in front of new Believers, especially being that many of these new Believers are just escaping a life of alcoholism and don't need to be presented again with the same temptations they just started to escape. The seasoned Believer, in an attempt to "keep it real" and prove to the world that he or she is still human, is actually misusing their liberty in Christ and exposing sinners and new Believers alike to information that will distract them from Christ. Remember: You are not the subject, the object everyone is supposed to be focusing on; Christ is. Put Christ on blast, not yourself. Don't fall into the trap of making yourself the main topic of discussion. You are not the issue to begin with; it's the souls of sinners and God's plan of salvation that should be the main topic. Move you out of the way and let Christ be lifted up.

King Solomon wrote in the Song of Solomon 2:7,

"Promise me, O women of Jerusalem, by the gazelles and wild deer, not to awaken love until the time is right" (NLT). Some versions may say, "Don't awaken love before its time." What this addresses is the fact that there are some things we, as individuals, don't need to know until we reach a period of maturity in our lives. For example, Solomon was revealing the danger of exposing children to subject matters of an adult nature. In other words, your 5 year-old doesn't need to be exposed to content of a sexual nature. Why? Because that's a form of awakening them to love "before its time." Sure, they'll come into the knowledge of sex and sexuality, but when it's the appropriate time to do so.

Some subject matters shouldn't be brought up during certain settings and events because it's not the appropriate time to bring them up. When having a family reunion, it isn't wise to bring up old wounds that haven't healed. This will undoubtedly turn what would have been an enjoyable get-together into a chaotic situation filled with fighting, cursing, and arguing. Don't mention that situation Aunt Flossy and Uncle Albert dealt with; it's going to make Cousin Anthony mad…and then all hell is going to break loose. Learn that some information, although important, shouldn't be brought up the moment it comes to your mind. The Bible says, "A fool uttereth all his mind: but a wise man keepeth it in till afterwards" (Proverbs 29:11). In the New Living Translation, it reads, "Fools vent their anger, but the wise quietly hold it back." That's self-explanatory. A fool speaks his or her mind the second something irks or bothers them, while a wise person practices concealing their tongue, holding back their words, not sharing their feelings and displaying their emotions in certain situations; and might I add, not bringing up subject matters that they know are going to enrage and inflame others when not necessary. It's just not the right time. Now is not the time to show everyone your Winnie-the-Poo pajamas, or let the world in on your argument with your wife over the household chores or the in-laws. Now is not the time nor the place to have cameras follow you to the lounge and show you drinking alcohol while smoking cigars and discussing politics and faith. It's just not the right time nor the place for that.

OVEREXPOSURE

Anything that is overexposed will ultimately become damaged or will die. For example, you become overexposed to too much sunlight and become dehydrated or develop skin cancer. To be honest, too much of anything can be damaging to you. The Bible even tells us in Ecclesiastes to avoid being "overly righteous," which means don't be so spiritual that you can no longer relate with others; don't act as if you live in the heavens and aren't currently residing on planet earth. You still have bills to pay. You still have needs that must be met. You still need food, clothing…intimacy and companionship. In other words, Solomon is telling you to stop running around claiming Jesus is your boyfriend and saying you don't "need nobody" but Jesus. That's a lie. You secretly crave having a warm body in the bed beside you at night, someone to go to out to eat and to the movies with on the weekends; you need someone to talk to, to connect with, receive love and affection from, etc. Yes, you are human. Keep things in balance. The Apostle Paul explained in 1 Corinthians chapter seven that married people must balance out their time spent in church and at home and avoid neglecting the marriage bed and time spent at home. He explained that spending too much time focusing on the things of the house of God may lead to neglecting your marriage and household. You can be in church too much and let your marriage die or too little and let your spirit man die. Balance is key. Not too much. Not too little. The same thing goes for transparency.

Now, keeping this in mind, what things should we be transparent with? Well, being transparent about your church's giving is a good thing. Letting people see where their money is going is not a bad thing; this establishes trust and credibility in your ministry and gives the members a greater level of confidence as it pertains to giving. If you have a building project going on, then it helps to have a building fund. By establishing a building fund, you're showcasing before your entire congregation what your future plans are, you're giving them a visual image of what they're giving to (the Bible tells us that without a vision the people will "perish," which means "to be scattered"), and you're including them in on the process. That's a good thing. As leaders in the church, we should strive to model before others an example of righteousness, but in the process there's nothing wrong with sharing with others our struggles to do so. I can't say that, for example, The Preachers of LA was critically damaging, although there were certain things I would find it unnecessary to air on television. There were a lot of great moments. To show the behind-the-scenes activities in preparation for major crusades and ministry events was actually beneficial. Sometimes, the streets need to know that it takes a lot of money to pull off ministry events. Sometimes, people in and out of the church need to be exposed to the amount of work, time, and energy that goes into planning conferences, they need to see the struggle to get funding just to continue with outreach activities and programs; they need to see the struggle. It's interesting that the Bible reveals to us the struggles that every man and woman of God faced. The Bible makes it clear that Moses wrestled with a temper and even committed murder, that King Solomon and King David were womanizers who dealt with lust issues, that the Prophet Noah wrestled with alcoholism (he got drunk immediately after the flood), that the Prophet Jonah wrestled with obeying God in all matters, that the Apostle Peter had a bad temper and was prone to fits of violence when agitated, that King Hezekiah had a tendency to brag too much on his possessions, that Joseph was gifted but very naive, that the Prophet Samuel had a tendency to take rejection too personally, etc. God, through His own Word, strives to show us the struggles of each man and woman of faith so that we can connect with them on a more personal and intimate level. Regardless of where we come from, all of us struggle in life. The rich struggle to hold on to their wealth while the poor struggle to gain wealth. The unemployed struggles to get a job while the employed struggles to meet deadlines and remain employed. Even Jesus, as revealed by Hebrews chapter five, had to struggle and learn how to be obedient so that He could become the author and finisher of our faith. The Bible even makes a point of mentioning that Jesus struggled with temptation, being that He was "tempted in all points" as we are. Apparently, God believes it's a beneficial thing to showcase certain struggles. But it is unnecessary to show-case struggles that don't add to one's witness for Christ and doesn't point men to Christ. You can let people know that you have struggles without sharing every little detail. Learn to be discreet about some things and avoid letting everyone in on personal information they don't need to know. For example, you can let people know you're wrestling with a health issue, but you don't have to give them the diagnoses and share with them how it began, etc. You don't even have to tell them what it is. Just say, "I'm wrestling with some health issues right now. Pray for me." Everyone doesn't need to know every little detail about what you're going through. Save the details for individuals you can confide in. When tes-tifying before a congregation or before strangers, don't tell all of your personal business. If you're husband cheated on you, don't get up and say in front of everyone, "Yeah. My husband was cheating on me with that little floozy right there on pew number two." Be discreet about some things. You can simply say, "My husband and I were going through some things; we encountered a situation in our marriage that was a true test of our love, but we overcame it by the grace of God. Con-tinue to pray for us." No one needs to know it was Becky… with the good hair. If you share too much information, this will stir up more tension in the house as people who have no business being involved in your marriage will begin to add more pressure to an already existing problem. It's better to keep others out of some things lest they complicate matters even more. Too many people being involved with distract you from the real problem at hand and hinder, or even kill, the healing process.

Notice in Scripture that God gives men a "measure of faith." By measure, the Bible is revealing to us that God knows how to give us just enough to keep us going but not enough to weigh us down. God gives us just enough revelation to inspire and motivate us, but He doesn't overwhelm and discourage us with the big picture. God will give us a small glimpse of our future through a prophetic word, but He won't show us everything, nor will He reveal to us all of the things we'll have to face just to get there. If God shows us too much, we'll try to get to our places of destiny without Him; so He shows us only enough to wet our appetites keeps us in the position to continually rely and depend on Him for His guidance in getting there and His protection along the way. What messed man up in the Garden of Eden was his desire to know more than he needed to know in the quest to shake off his dependency on God. God knows how much is too much.

DRAMA

When dealing with Millennials today, it is important to remember that we're dealing with a group who has been overexposed to the private lives of public figures. This overexposure to information that is inconsequential has developed within an appetite in many within today's generation to fish for information that isn't conducive for spiritual growth and necessary for their personal and spiritual development. It's true that many people are drawn to drama. Yes, many people like to see drama and mess. Some people won't tune in to a show unless there's some type of drama going on. If there's going to be a reality TV show on air, its producers are going to make sure they identify the drama-king or drama-queen and urge them on and give them as much screen time as possible; participants on the show who're unwilling to be swept up in a hailstorm of controversy and drama are usually phased out of the production and replaced in the following seasons. Reality TV thrives on drama. Connoisseurs of reality TV thrive on drama: they don't tune in to what's going on until or unless there's some drama involved. Whenever pastors are featured on the news for some type of scandal, that's when many people will tune-in. People love to pay attention to the drama that goes on in the church. You can't stop that nor change that. When the news talks about a pastor and his wife getting into a fist fight in a public parking lot, that's when the world starts talking. When a pastor is being investigated for sexual misconduct and/or the misuse of church funds, that's when all eyes will be on that church. One local Bishop, while embroiled in a national scandal over sexual misconduct allegations, found his church service being overrun on Sunday mornings (not even any standing room left) not by people who wanted to worship at his establishment, but by nosy spectators who wanted to find out if the allegations were true. Some people only show up to watch another reality TV showdown in the church.

The Bible says in Proverbs 17:4, "Wrongdoers eagerly listen to gossip; liars pay close attention to slander" (NLT). Solomon said people who have corrupt and perverse natures look for perverse and corrupt things. Why do wrongdoers fiend for bad news about others, including ministers and public figures, to come out? It's because hearing about someone else's wrongdoing justifies their own wrongdoings in their minds. Oftentimes, whenever confronting someone who is living in sin about their actions and activities, they'll bring up the sins of famous pastors and Christian leaders in their defense; this is their shield, their defense against conviction and the feeling of guilt. Any sin that a person seeks to justify, they don't intend to repent of.

It's imperative that we, as the Body of Christ, not curve the message of the Gospel, which not only entails salvation through Christ but repentance from sin, just to appeal to people, regardless or whether they're Millennials or not. You're not going to reach everyone with the Gospel. Some people will only show up to church or tune-in to what's going on in a church if there's something negative happening there, but there are others who genuinely want to hear sound doctrine and have an experience with God because they sense an internal void that can only be filled with the presence of God in their lives. Focus on those who're hungry for God, not those who're hungry for drama while helping those hungry for God to remain focused on God rather than distracted by personal, petty problems. As in every generation, there is a remnant of hungry people who're desperate for God, for the truth, for the presence and anointing of God in their lives; you just have to focus on lifting Christ up.

THE NEED FOR WISDOM

Ultimately, in the end, we must rely on the Holy Spirit's guidance when determining what to disclose and when and how much to the public as God's people, especially as leaders. It was the Holy Spirit who guided the Apostle Paul in what and what not to say when standing before others. Likewise, the Holy Spirit is here to be our guide. He knows how much is too much or too little. He knows what should be shared and what needs to remain concealed and hidden. Wisdom dictates that we take every matter to God in prayer and ask Him for guidance on what to say, what to share, what not to say or share, and even how to say or share what we're supposed to say or share. Without this wisdom, we're highly likely to say the wrong things at the wrong time and reveal things to the wrong people that may be damaging to their spiritual development. We have to have a love in our hearts for God's people, one that will temper our words and direct our motives whenever speaking to them. God will reveal to you your motives in every situation. He'll let you see if your motives are driven by material things such as money, or if you're driven by fleshly ambitions.

I can't honestly say to you it's right or wrong to become a part of a reality TV show. I can't say you should or you shouldn't. All I can say to you is you must first ask the Holy Spirit to guide you in the matter, ask God to check your motives, and make sure you're walking in-sync with God's will. Maybe God will tell you to get on the show. Maybe He'll use you mightily on that platform. Maybe God has a special blessing in store for you in that arena, by being on that show. Only God knows. Only God. But one thing is for sure: When money and fame are your motivating factors, you lack the wisdom to know how much is too much.

CHAPTER FOUR

BECOMING RELEVANT AGAIN

THE BIGGEST DANGER TODAY'S CHURCH FACES IS THE danger of becoming irrelevant. The word *relevant* means "closely connected or appropriate to what is being done or considered; appropriate to the current time, period, or circumstances; of contemporary interest" (www.Dictionary.com). With this definition, *irrelevance* means *to be disconnected with the activities and issues that matter the most to society at the moment.* So, when I say the church wrestles today with remaining relevant, I mean the modern church, by and large, is behind the curve when it comes to appealing to Millennials and setting the moral standard in society. In other words, Millennials don't look to the church for guidance in matters of morality. When it comes to politics, the church practically has little to no influence on the voting direction of Millennials; it has little to no influence on the political decisions being made in Washington. I'm not saying there are no God-fearing political leaders in our nation; I'm saying there are significantly fewer today than in times past. Although the first public school began in a church in this country, today, the church has no influence in our public schools; in fact, there is an anti-Christian campaign currently ravaging our schools, creating an atmosphere where teachers and coaches may find themselves being fired for doing simple things like bringing a Bible to class, having Christian literature on their desks during class time, or praying before a football or basketball game. When it comes to the mainstream media, the church has little influence on the content created and promoted in Hollywood. The blockbuster hit film *The Passion of the Christ*, produced by Mel Gibson, stunned Hollywood because it revealed to them that there is a large Christian audience that desires to see biblically-based films, but Mel Gibson had to produce the film using his own money. And since then, Hollywood has fired back with films perverting and twisting the Christian message such as *Noah*, starring Russel Crowe, *Exodus: Gods and Kings* starring Christian Bale, and shows like *Black Jesus* where they depict Jesus as a weed-smoking, foul-mouthed, fornicating individual. These are the films non-church-goers gain their theological perspective from. Rather than go to the church to hear the truth about Jesus during Bible study, most Millennials would rather read Dan Brown's bestseller *Da Vinci Code*, which claims Jesus fled to Europe and got married to one of His female disciples, Mary Magdalene, and had children by her, and His bones are currently being held by the Catholic Church.

Today, when you look at Europe, most of the churches that once stood and thrived there sit empty—some dilapidated, rundown, in ruins. The ones that are standing idle have been turned into Mosques and temples for modern pagan worship used by Wiccans and other occult groups. In Canada, many churches lie abandoned as well. Today, in America, there is an epidemic of empty congregations as churches struggle just to get the people through the doors throughout the week and on Sundays. All of this points to one thing: the church is becoming irrelevant in the eyes of today's generation; and hence, it's becoming obsolete. Millennials don't see the church as important today, as necessary, as needed. But why?

LOSING RELEVANCY

Before I can talk about how the church can become relevant again, I need to address the key reasons why the church has lost its relevancy in today's culture. First off, when you ask many Baby-Boomers why the youth don't look to the church as the source of information and the moral authority in the land, they'll fire back with excuses like these: "These young folks just ain't been through nothing. They don't know what hard times look like. Let them go through something and they'll run back to God." "It's the devil that got these young folk's minds. They too worldly." Well, let's look at these two statements: Regarding the claim that Millennials haven't gone through anything, that's not true. Young people in this society, despite Baby-Boomers' attempts to shield them from the dangers of the outside world, find themselves dealing with much stress, many of them unemployed while burdened with debt; and as I mentioned at the beginning of this book, they have more to worry about. The world is no safer today than it was before; in fact, there are greater dangers looming. Who would have ever imagined forty, fifty years ago that nuclear annihilation would be a global threat? Who would have worried forty, fifty years ago about a Electro Magnetic Pulse bomb (EMP) devastating the nation, thrusting us back into the Stone Age? Who would have imagined having to face new strains of diseases that seemingly have no cure? And there's so much more. Racism is just as vibrant today in our society as it was in days past. Mass murder and mass shootings in public places has become commonplace in our society. No, I can't say Millennials don't face the same challenges their parents faced because they do face those same challenges—and some.

Now, regarding the statement that the devil has the minds of today's youth, I want to ask you one question: Why has Satan become so successful? If Jesus gave the church the keys (authority) of the Kingdom of Heaven to tread on the heads of devils, why then is Satan so successful in entrapping the minds of the youth? Why does a defeated foe have so much power over the church in today's culture? How did Satan gain an advantage over the church? Yes, Satan is the culprit, but who let him in the room? Who gave him the power and authority to do what he does? With that in mind, the true blame lies with the church, not the devil. How has the church given Satan so much clout with Millennials? It has done so by keeping its mouth shut while Satan was on the move in our society. Many Believers today remain silent while politicians make policies that violate God's laws, and they claim "separation of church and state" when you ask them why they refuse to raise their voices concerning political matters. In the 1950s and 1960s, when the Supreme Court was banning prayer and Bibles from public schools and promoting Evolution and abortion, the church pretty much stayed silent and quietly prayed and hoped for a change rather than cry aloud and speak up for the truth.

You can't defeat an enemy you refuse to fight. Regarding the church today, due to our insistence on remaining silent in the face of the Adversary's activities, Satan has been given more power and authority over our culture and society. And sadly, while Satan has his way with the world around us, the church remains distracted with its own petty issues. The church is embroiled in an internal fight over whether or not women should be allowed to preach and pastor, or whether or not worship leaders should be allowed to wear jeans during worship service, or whether or not Holy Hip Hop and Christian rock bands should be allowed into the church, or whether or not worship services should be held on Saturdays or Sundays. The Apostle Paul explained in Romans chapter fourteen,

"Accept other believers who are weak in faith, and don't argue with them about what they think in right or wrong.... Who are you to condemn someone else's servants? Their own master will judge whether they stand or fall. And with the Lord's help, they will stand and receive his approval. In the same way, some think one day is more holy than another day, while others think every day is alike. You should each be fully convinced that whichever day you choose is acceptable" (vs. 1, 4, 5, NLT).

The Apostle Paul went on to say,

> "For the Kingdom of God is not a matter of what we eat or drink, but of living a life of goodness and peace and joy in the Holy Spirit. If you serve Christ with this attitude, you will please God, and others will approve of you, too. So then, let us aim for harmony in the church and try to build each other up. Don't tear apart the work of God over what you eat. Remember, all foods are acceptable, but it is wrong to eat something if it makes another person stumble." (17-20, NLT)

Notice Paul's plea to the church to not "tear apart the work of God" over what he considered to be petty differences in opinion about how the worship service should go. As he stated, we shouldn't argue over what "day" we think is holier, but rather choose as individuals to honor God on whatever day we choose ("be fully convinced that whichever day you choose is acceptable"). We shouldn't get caught up in arguments small cultural nuances such as the style of music one prefers to express their worship with (Holy Hip Hop, Rock, Country, Traditional, Opera, etc.); or as Paul dealt with in his day, the issue of food—the type of food one eats, whether or not that food was sacrificed to an idol, etc. In essence, Paul would eat whatever food was placed in front of him regardless of who it was sacrificed to. Why? Because Paul stated that he'd simply pray over the food and dedicate it to God, which would make it fine in his sight after that.

Regarding women preaching in the church, Paul

wrote in Galatians 3:27-29,

> "For as many of you as have been baptized into Christ
> have put on Christ. There is neither Jew nor Greek,
> there is neither bond nor free, there is neither male nor
> female: for ye are all one in Christ Jesus. And if ye be
> Christ's, then are ye Abraham's seed, and heirs accord-
> ing to the promise."

Here, the Apostle Paul explained that all of us as Believers
are anointed and have the responsibility of "put on Christ,"
which means to wear the character of Christ, live a life of god-
liness, and surrender our bodies as vessels of the Holy Spirit
to use to reach the lost. Paul tells Christians to take off their
individual identities (male, female, Jew, gentile, free, bond,
Black, White, rich, poor, educated, uneducated, short, tall,
etc.) and wear only one identity when it comes to the work
of ministry: Christ. By this, Paul was saying Christ is the
center of attention, the one calling the shots, the one who is
sovereign enough to use whomever He chooses. Christ can
use a man, a woman, even a child (remember the Prophet
Jeremiah?) or a donkey (remember the Prophet Balaam?).
We should, therefore, stop judging God's chosen vessels and
listen to the message being presented by those vessels. Until
we stop fighting each other for supremacy, arguing over issues that have no bearing on our souls' salvation, Satan will
continue to run amok unopposed. Furthermore, Millennials
will witness all of the infighting in the church over issues
that don't mean anything to them and continue to walk in
the opposite direction. They don't care about the petty is-

sues most church-goers fight over. These are the issues they're looking at today:

THE ISSUES

Sexuality. Racism and injustice. The problem of suffering in our world. The economy. The truth about the unseen, invisible, spiritual realm of existence. These are some of the main issues that the youth are concerned about today. While the church fights over whether or not Sunday or Saturday should be the day of worship, the youth are trying to figure out whether or not gender roles should be recognized and exist, whether or not it is a violation of civil liberties for society to avoid recognizing the legitimacy of same-sex unions, whether or not babies are humans while in the womb, whether or not there will be jobs available for them once they graduate from college with a ton of student loan debt on their shoulders, whether or not they should try Wicca (witchcraft) and use magic to get what they want in life, and they're trying to understand the reality of the spiritual realm—what are ghosts, should we consult with spirit guides, are we gods, etc. In order to remain relevant, you must present the answers to today's questions, you must meet the world where it is rather than expect the world to come to where you are.

Are you prepared to answer the questions of today? Are you prepared to minister to the issues of today? What would you do if two men walked into your church holding hands, or a lesbian couple joined your congregation, or a transgender person joined your church and desires to sing on your praise team? How would you handle this new reality? How will you minister to a man who may have more estrogen than testosterone in his body and uses this as the bases to support his alternative sexual lifestyle? Is the church ready to handle the tide of new questions prompted by new scientific discoveries? Are we ready to handle the people with the tough questions? If you run these people away, you'll be chasing the Millennial crowd out of your church, and rendering your church irrelevant. With Millennials today, you have the transgenders, you have the cohabiting couples who've been together for years but won't marry, you have the single parents whose children were born out of wedlock, you have the unemployed college graduates who just don't have the money to give although willing to serve where they can, you have girls who've had multiple abortions, you have porn stars, the strippers, the drug dealers, the drug addicts, kids whose influences are rap artists with tattoos and gold teeth and wild hairstyles, and more. You must know your audience. You must understand their issues and concerns. You must be willing to let them speak and provide the answers to their questions.

REGAINING RELEVANCY

Culture and society are constantly changing. You might as well get with the times. Technology isn't going anywhere, so you might as well get acclimated to it and learn how to use it. You won't be able to compete with the world for the attention of the youth if you're lagging behind in the areas of technology in your church. If you notice that young people today spend more time on social media than anything else, why aren't you on Facebook, Instagram, Twitter, etc. promoting your ministry and the Gospel message? Jesus told

Peter he was going to become a "fisher of men." As a fisher-man, Peter knew what that meant: he would have to get on a boat and go out into the water to where the fish were, and he would have to cast the net in the water to trap the fish, understanding that they weren't going to jump out of the water and flop around on the land until finally making their way into Peter's refrigerator. You have to go to where the fish are. They're not coming to you.

Perhaps, it's a blow to the pride of Baby-boomer Christians that they have to work to catch Millennials and wield them back into the church. Perhaps, many church-go-ers just assume that Millennials are going to go to church out of tradition, but tradition is fading. It's important to note that there are so many more options available to Mil-lennials today in terms of religion. Today, Millennials can easily assimilate into the New Age Spirituality Movement floating around and immerse themselves in mind-sciences and esoteric practices while enjoying the comforts of their home. Today, they can pull up any preacher, guru, tantric, imam, etc. on Youtube and have a religious experience right from their living room. Technology has brought the world to their fingers. Is your voice represented? When the Apostle Paul went to Athens in Greece and visited Mars Hill, he no-ticed there were hundreds of monuments dedicated to idol gods there, but he also noticed one with the inscription "To the unknown god" on it and he seized the opportunity to use that one opening to share the Gospel. Paul didn't try to knock down the other monuments; he simply took advan-tage of an opening. Yes, the venue is crowded online. There are plenty of options to compete with, but being absent from the scene doesn't increase your chances of reaching the lost; it decreases them. You have to utilize the current technological platforms that are being used by the masses to get your message out there. Social media is beginning to replace television. According to the BBC, "Social media has overtaken television as young people's main source of news, according to a report."[1]

In 1955, Robert H. Schuller, a Christian evangelist living in California, had a ingenious idea. He wanted to build a church, an audience, a congregation, so he decided to go to where the people were: the Orange County Drive-In Theater. He decided to have church at the Drive-In theater rather than waiting for movie-goers to venture to his church. His plan worked. People were glad to drive their cars to the drive-in, park them there, turn on their radios, and enjoy Dr. Schuller's sermons from the comforts of their vehicles... while chucking down hamburgers and fries and milkshakes. It was this pool of attendees who later became his congregation, helping him to build the famous Crystal Cathedral in California. He went to where the people were. He caught fish. Likewise, if we are going to remain relevant in today's society, we must go to where the fish are, we must go to where the issues are, we must go to where the popular social platforms are, we must raise our voices and share God's heart as it pertains to the pertinent issues of the day.

Again, Millennials don't go to church out of tradition. They have too many other options. You have to attract Millennials to your church. The way to do this is to have the right appeal, the right atmosphere, address the issues and concerns they carry and preach the pure Gospel, one that's not polluted with manmade traditions that lessen its effectiveness.

CHAPTER FIVE

TO CATCH A FISH

IN OUR PREVIOUS CHAPTER, I ADDRESSED THE ISSUE OF irrelevancy and what primarily causes it. Now, I want to go a little deeper in how to regain relevancy and reach Millennials. As we discussed in the last chapter, Jesus told His disciples that He would teach them how to become "fishers of men" in Matthew 4:19. Jesus was using an analogy these men would easily understand being that they were fishermen. They understood the ropes. They knew how to fish. They knew the process. Of course, using this same analogy today, many of us understand what Jesus meant when He called us "fishers of men." We understand that it requires patience, the proper technique, the proper tools, and so much more to catch a fish. The same techniques that apply to fishing are the same techniques that apply to evangelism. It amazes me when I see Christians scrambling over what methods to use to draw young people to their churches when Jesus already provided for us the formula. If we'd simply follow the advice Jesus gave us, we'd find our evangelistic efforts being a lot more fruitful. Unfortunately, for many within the church who suffer selective amnesia, we must be reminded of the evangelistic formula, of the process of fishing.

YOU CAN'T CATCH FISH WITH KNIVES

There's an old saying that goes, "You can't clean a fish until you first catch it." One of the biggest problems many Christians have when it comes to evangelizing Millennials is they believe it necessary to "clean-up" the person's outer appearance before introducing them to the cross. We want the person to change their image, stop sagging their pants, get rid of their tattoos, take out their gold grills, stop smoking weed, stop rolling blunts, stop twerking, stop desiring same-sex relationships, stop being angry, stop being ratchet, stop dressing like a stripper, get rid of their fake butts and fake boobs, stop cursing; we want the males to take the earrings off, we want the females to remove their tongue rings, we want Millennials to completely give-up the world, change their appearances, clean-up their acts, change their attitudes, become reverent, pious, God-fearing, abhor sinful practices, develop humble spirits, turn their backs on wickedness and iniquity, look and act like perfect little angels before we begin to embrace them, evangelize them, disciple them, minister to them, and pray with them. That's backward. It's backward to seek to clean the fish, to gut the fish and bring about a transformation in its life before first catching the fish.

Maybe there's a fear that resides in the hearts of many Christians that if they were to open their doors to all of the fish waiting on the outside, they'd be unprepared to deal with the issues those fish bring. Some Christians are afraid to let the ratchet girls and the strippers and dancers into their pretty little churches for fear that the deacons might lose their sanity and their salvation—as well as the ministers. Because of this, in many churches, whenever a young, beautiful, well-shaped girl enters the church, I've seen older ladies look at her with condemning eyes, treat her with scorn, act cold towards her, and even chase her out of the church for fear that she might tempt too many men. Not only does the young lady have to worry about the lustful men, but she has to worry about the insecure women present; and, at the end of the day, hanging in the balance is that young lady's eternal, precious soul. The men couldn't see past their lusts and the ladies couldn't see past their insecurities and behold a soul in need, standing before them, one that Jesus died to save. Insecure and intimidated Christians then pull out their knives in hopes that the young lady will yield herself to be cleaned and gutted before even being transformed by the Gospel. Many church-goers fear their church being overrun with people they can't control, people that don't think and act like them, people that don't look like them and share their same mentalities. But thank God that Jesus didn't act this way. I'm glad Jesus didn't make Christianity a country club requiring a certain dress-code, a certain economic status, and level of education. Jesus opened the doors of His church to "whosoever" that would come, and He wasn't afraid of who came because He had enough power to change anyone's heart and banish anyone's demons, and He had enough love in His heart to help heal anyone's wounds, and He had enough revelation to answer anyone's questions and bring peace to anyone's mind. Jesus wasn't afraid to receive every type of fish because He was equipped to deal with every type of fish.

Yes, it's true. The people that followed Christ weren't perfect angels. They were people like Mary Magdalene, a street woman who had been possessed by seven demons, and Peter, an impetuous fisherman with a quick temper who was prone to acts of violence. Jesus received a lot of criticism for associating with people like Zacchaeus, a tax collector who was a well-known thief and turncoat that preyed on his own kind and was hated by his own kind. Jesus also caught a lot of flak for having a conversation with a half-breed, a Samaritan woman at a well one day—this was culturally forbidden by the Jews who considered the Samaritans to be beneath them due to their bloodline. I must admit that between women who wrestled with demonic possession (sexual demons, perverse demons, demons of anger, etc.) and fishermen with intense anger issues and corrupt government employees who loved to abuse their authority, not to mention dishonest, untrustworthy activists like Judas and overly skeptical men like Thomas, Jesus rolled with an interesting group. The members of Jesus' entourage wouldn't be well-received by the majority of today's churches. They wouldn't even be allowed through the doors of many churches today. In today's culture, a *Mary Magdalene* would walk through the doors of the church dressed in her hooker heels, wearing a mini-skirt, and having her cleavage hanging out, wearing long weave and a lot of makeup, acting ratchet while being possessed by multiple demons, and the religious ladies in the church would simply sneer, criticize, scorn, roll their eyes, and cast shade at her rather than embrace her with open arms as Jesus did and minister to her and pray with her. Today, a *Peter* would enter into the sanctuary stinking, filthy, dirty, and tense, ready to snap on anyone that crosses him the wrong way, always "packing" (carrying a weapon), and the ushers and deacons would miss half of the service for staring at him out of the corners of their eyes and waiting for any occasion to escort him out of the building. I can only imagine if a *Zacchaeus* dared try to enter the church. His tarnished reputation would permeate the air like a foul odor. He'd be enshrouded by a haze of whispers. Contempt for him would show on everyone's faces. No one would want to sit next to him, greet him at any point during the service, be seen standing next to him or talking to him, join hands with him during the service, nor see him walk down the aisle and join the church during the altar call. Jesus' earthly cousin, John the Baptist, wouldn't be allowed into the sanctuary. That guy walked around dressed like a thug and he ate crickets with raw honey while rambling on as if delusional. At the entrance of the church, a few of the deacons would stop him and redirect him to the eighth floor of Grady Hospital where he'd receive psychological treatment—perhaps be placed on medication, antidepressants, maybe Abilify to treat Schizophrenia. And how could I leave out Legion? He's too intense for even the crack-house. Even the dope-boys don't want him around. No one wants him in their pews. The only place people want to see him in is a psych ward wearing a straight jacket. He can't even enter the prison and hang out with the general population. And yet, Jesus entered right into Legion's backyard, confronted him with the power of God, cast all of the demons out of him—thousands of them—and then brought him right back to himself (clothed and in his right mind).

Jesus did that for everyone that He met. He didn't criticize them for how they looked; He understood why they acted the way they acted, and He didn't feel intimidated by their sins and conditions; instead, He came armed and equipped with the love and power of God to set them free. After being set free from the grip of darkness, each of these individuals began to change the way they carried themselves on their own. Jesus never had to tell Mary to cover up. He didn't have to tell Legion to put some clothes on. You don't read in the Gospels where Jesus preached to Legion about the importance of not sagging his pants and cutting himself. Jesus did spend His time dealing with *symptoms*; He addressed the root issue: the spirit man. When the demons tormenting Legion were gone, Legion was finally back in his "right mind" and was now aware of the fact that he needed some clothes on. I'm not saying there's no need for simple instructions on how to dress appropriately. What I am saying is each of the fish Jesus caught was more than eager to put on decent clothes, pull their pants up, and look presentable because they'd been hooked by the love and power of God.

If a person doesn't first feel loved and accepted enough by you, they'll never trust you enough to let you clean them up. The people who followed Jesus trusted Him because they knew He loved them. Jesus won their hearts; and hence, He won their trust. Each of Jesus' followers knew He accepted them; and furthermore, they were drawn to the light of the Father, which shined brightly through Christ. Each of Jesus' followers saw in Jesus something they desired to have, that which they all lacked, and therefore, longed for: peace, joy, true happiness, pure love, internal freedom, favor with the Father; and unadulterated power. Jesus wasn't moved by fear and insecurity when dealing with others; He was moved by compassion. When we truly love others and desire to see them healed, whole, and walking in the perfect will of God for their lives, we won't be deterred by their outer appearances when reaching out to them; we won't make tattoos and nose-rings such a big issue; instead, we'll be driven by the urgency to get them to the cross so that God can do an internal work in their lives, save the souls, and transform their hearts. Only after this will the fish be prepared to be cleaned.

WHERE'S YOUR BAIT?

Let's face it, some people aren't that skilled at fishing. They aren't. Some people ignore one of the cardinal rules of fishing: You must use the right bait to catch the desired type of fish. For example, the best bait to use when fishing for bass are crickets; worms also work well with them. For most fish, Minnows work well. However, for white fish, wax worms work the best, although bigger fish aren't attracted to them. If you're in the Gulf of Mexico, you'll notice fishermen using squid to catch snappers and other big fish. However, there is one thing I can tell you no fish is attracted to: a big shiny silver hook. Jesus would use parables to hook the Jews attention, realizing that if He gave them the raw, naked truth, they'd be unable to digest it. In Hebrews 5:14, the Bible tells us that some information is too hard for new Believers to handle—it's like trying to feed a baby with no teeth a cheap steak. Some people have to mature to the level of handling certain revelations and information. So, Jesus used a simple bait to catch His target audience; and being that this particular audience was comprised of fishermen and shepherds, Jesus used analogies they'd be used to in His parables: fishing, farming, agricultural symbols, etc. What bait are you using? Parables (short stories)? Entertainment such as plays and other productions? Music? If so, what kind? Programs aimed to aide and assist the needs of the needy? Your talents and gifts?

Certain things attract Millennials. To tell you the truth, what worked for grandma won't entice today's generation, especially in light of the many alternatives out there. If your church is in "da' hood" then featuring Christian rock bands or Christian country western artists to perform on Sundays probably won't attract those in your community. If everyone in your neighborhood is listening to hip-hop and R&B, then Christian artists that carry that particular flavor in their music would be more appealing. You have to speak the language of a community if you're going to attract the people in that community. When we look at the Black Church, there is a divide between the Baby-Boomers and Millennials in terms of the music, style of dress, and culture. For example, Millennials don't necessarily want to hear "I'm just a poor pilgrim of sorrow" or "Lo down chariot". Those are great hymns and spirituals, but they're not appealing to the crowd that listens to "Goochie Gang". Millennials are not going to be drawn to churches that don't speak their language. In today's culture, Millennials tend to be entrepreneurs who're used to conducting business from the laptops, cell-phones and tablets while wearing jeans and t-shirts; so, should it be any surprise that they'd want a more casual feel in church? No, it shouldn't. They go to their offices at work in jeans and blazers (or sports jackets). Of course, not all of them. But most do. Now, if your goal is to reach a different crowd, then it's important that you "look the part" and create that type of environment and culture in your church. Know the culture your church is surrounded by and mirror it. Just don't let the Gospel message mirror the culture. You can still preach that Jesus is the only way to heaven while wearing blue jeans and a blazer or t-shirt. You can sing the Gospel or rap the Gospel; either way, at least the message, which is the real issue, is getting out.

The Apostle Paul stated in 1 Corinthians 9:22,

"And unto the Jews I became as a Jew, that I might gain the Jews; to them that are under the law, as under the law, that I might gain them that are under the law; to them that are without law, as without law, (being not without law to God, but under the law to Christ,) that I might gain them that are without law. To the weak became I as weak, that I might gain the weak: I am made all things to all men, that I might by all means save some."

In the New Living Translation, this reads,

"When I was with the Jews, I lived like a Jew to bring the Jews to Christ. When I was with those who follow the Jewish law, I too lived under that law. Even though I am not subject to the law, I did this so I could bring to Christ those who are under the law. When I am with the Gentiles who do not follow the Jewish law, I too live

85

apart from that law so I can bring them to Christ. But I do not ignore the law of God; I obey the law of Christ. When I am with those who are weak, I share their weakness, for I want to bring the weak to Christ. Yes, I try to find common ground with everyone, doing everything I can to save some."

You can call the Apostle Paul "Mr. International". He would go into a different city, become familiar with the culture and the people of that land, and then begin to evangelize them with the Gospel while using their own cultural nuances. For example, in Acts 16:3, the Bible tells us that the Apostle Paul, the very person who taught against the doctrine that the physical circumcision was a prerequisite for salvation, required that his son in the ministry, Timothy, get circumcised before ministering to the Jews simply because he knew the Jews would not receive the ministry of an uncircumcised man. The circumcision had nothing to do with Timothy's salvation; it did, however, have much to do with Timothy's ability to appeal to a particular group of people. Paul did whatever it took to reach different cultures. He wasn't bound to any culture, but he was sensitive to every culture's beliefs and practices. He'd do his homework before entering into a new territory. How many evangelicals are today educating themselves on the latest cultural nuances in their own backyard? As a Baby-boomer, you don't have to use the slang that Millennials use, but it would help to understand the meanings of their slang terminology if not for any other reason but to show them you're hip to their game. Little things like this gain the attention of the younger generation and show them that you're interested in knowing and understanding them. Paul wanted to relate to his audience. God, in an attempt to relate to us better, put on flesh and dwelled among us as a man just so that He could boast this: "And he (Jesus) is able to deal gently with ignorant and wayward people because he himself is subject to the same weaknesses" (Hebrews 5:2, NLT). Jesus wanted to be able to relate to us, which is one of the reasons He came down from heaven and dwelled among us.

Being relatable is key to evangelizing the lost and reaching a lost generation, but this requires stepping outside of your comfort-zone and studying the fish so that you can grab the right type of bait. You have to become familiar with the group you're trying to reach and learn to speak their language. Why are ex-drug addicts so effective in reaching drug addicts? Why are ex-strippers so effective in evangelizing strippers and dancers? Why are ex-inmates so effective in evangelizing jails and prisons? It's because they can speak the language of these individuals. They understand the culture each of these individuals lives in. They know how they think. They understand how they feel. They can relate to them. Now, I'm not saying that a person who has never used drugs before can't witness and minister to a drug addict. Actually, there are plenty of ex-users who're sitting under the tutelage and guidance of men and women who've never walked down the path of addiction before. But somewhere along the way, the tutor and mentor become familiar with the specific challenges of the ex-user and remains conscious of these things. To become relatable, all you have to do is study the individual(s) you're trying to reach and become familiar with their challenges, struggles, feelings, emotions, and thoughts.

If you're reaching out to the homeless, your bait should be food, clothing, and shelter (in a sense, food works for any group. People will show up to church to eat). You need to be able to provide certain of their basic needs before they'll listen to anything you have to say. James 2:14-16 tells us that it does no good to bid a person well and simply bless them with your words while overlooking their physical need for food and clothing and shelter. If you're reaching out to strippers and prostitutes, you need to find out why they do what they do. It's obvious that money—quick money—is an obvious reason, but what other factors could be motivating forces? Is it a lack of education and opportunities? Are they worried about their kids? Are they victims of human trafficking? Are they addicted to drugs? What are the other factors? Why are young men joining gangs? It's not as simple as saying "money." There's more to it. Is it a lack of a father-figure? Is it due to a fear of being bullied and victimized if they're not a part of a gang or clique? What are the motivations? Instead of being afraid of the fish, study them and discover what it takes to get their attention so that you can point them to the cross of Christ.

Another bait used to reach Millennials is the power of God. Many churches today overlook the importance of the charismatic gifts of the Holy Spirit. It amazes me how many church leaders and members will shun the supernatural gifts of God but then ask God for a supernatural miracle when the doctors give them bad news. I've even known preachers who preach against the anointing of God lay hands on members who were in the hospital fighting for their lives. God gave us His power for a reason. Jesus explained to us in John 14:12 (NLT),

> "I tell you the truth, anyone who believes in me will do the same works I have done, and even greater works, because I am going to be with the Father."

Notice that Jesus said "anyone who believes," which means this power is extended to all of Christ's followers, not just to the twelve disciples. If you believe in Christ, then God has extended to you His anointing so that you can do the same works Christ did in Scripture, and some. What works did Jesus do? Well, all throughout the New Testament we see Jesus performing supernatural signs and wonders such as healing people bound with sicknesses, opening blinded eyes, healing those who were paralyzed, casting out demons, prophesying, giving words of knowledge like He did to the woman at the well (John 4:1-42); He even multiplied two fish and five loaves of bread and fed over ten thousand people; He even raised the dead. Now, Jesus is not a liar. When He told us we'd do those same exact things, He meant it. We would, through the anointing of the Holy Ghost, heal the sick, open blinded eyes, heal mental disorders, rebuke cancer cells, heal paralyzed bodies, cast out demonic spirits, prophesy, speak words of knowledge and wisdom, multiply resources supernaturally, and even raise the dead. Remember: Jesus' fame spread throughout the land not due to His parables, but due to His miracles. People came from all over just to see the power of God in action. Millennials today are attracted to the supernatural; they want to see something, not merely hear something. It's because of the supernatural display of the power of God that evangelists like Marylin Hickey was able to preach the Gospel...in a mosque! Yes, that's unheard of! A woman preaching in a mosque?! It happened! Why? Because Muslim or not, Jew or not, Buddhist or not, Hindu or not, atheist or not, when your body is racked with pain and sickness is consuming you through and through, when your child or loved one is sick and the doctors don't know what else to do, you will find yourself being willing to call on God for a miracle. Evangelist Hickey was invited to preach the Gospel in a mosque because the people there were desperate for a supernatural touch for God, and they saw the anointing on her life and witnessed the miracles being performed through her ministry. People don't care about words when they're suffering; they care about action. Let the world see God in action in your church. It is because of the anointing that ex-Muslims like Dr. Nasir Saddiki became Christians. As Dr. Saddiki recounts in his testimony, while dying from a rare sickness, he called on the name of Allah and got no answer, but then Christ appeared to Him and He began to call on the name of Jesus and was instantly, miraculously healed. His testimony is similar to many others who've decided to follow Jesus after coming out of other religions after experiencing a supernatural touch from God. And if your church isn't walking in the supernatural in this day and time, you are behind the curve.

Although the Gospel message is able to appeal to all men—it's a one size fits all message—the method in which it is presented varies. The methodology is the bait used to communicate the Gospel. Some ministries get creative and present the Gospel message through plays and other theatrical productions. Many churches, such as the Hillsong Church in Australia, have become widely popular through their music ministry—their praise and worship sessions are like concerts; their presentation is top-notch. When you think about it, the Grammy's, the BET Awards, the Hip Hop Awards, the CMAs, etc. all focus on offering top-notch presentations in order to captivate Millennials, so why should the church continue to offer second-rate presentations and expect to captivate the minds of Millennials? With Millennials, the atmosphere is so critical. They want an atmosphere where they aren't being judged, but are being embraced. This isn't to say we embrace their sins, but we must embrace their individuality and uniqueness and allow them to be themselves while teaching them the Word of God, which will bring about a change in their hearts. Also, they don't want a good sermon and a sense of religious duty; they want an experience. Satan has mastered the art of presenting an experience, but Christians don't think it necessary to step up their game. Like I said in an earlier chapter, we want to upgrade our televisions, upgrade our automobiles, upgrade our appliances, upgrade our cell phones, upgrade the furniture in our homes, upgrade our wardrobes, and upgrade everything else but our churches and our worship experiences. And yet, God wants us to put all of our energy and effort into the worship experience. He wants us to be creative. Bring in the concert lights. Set up the backdrops. Get the high-tech equipment. You can even bring in a fog machine. More liturgical, conservative congregations don't mind building symphony pits and have a full orchestra play during worship. They understand the need for class, for an incredible presentation. Put your all into the worship experience and be consistent with it. Be as creative as you can. God wants us to sing a new song, not get settled with the old. God complained in Malachi 1:6-8 (NLT),

> The LORD of Heaven's Armies says to the priests: "A son honors his father, and a servant respects his master. If I am your father and master, where are the honor and respect I deserve? You have shown contempt for my name! "But you ask, 'How have we ever shown contempt for your name?' "You have shown contempt by offering defiled sacrifices on my altar. "Then you ask, 'How have we defiled the sacrifices?' "You defile them by saying the altar of the LORD deserves no respect. When you give blind animals as sacrifices, isn't that wrong? And isn't it wrong to offer animals that are crippled and diseased? Try giving gifts like that to your governor, and see how pleased he is!" says the LORD of Heaven's Armies.

God also complained in Isaiah 43:24,

> "Thou hast bought me no sweet cane with money, neither hast thou filled me with the fat of thy sacrifices: but thou hast made me to serve with thy sins, thou hast wearied me with thine iniquities."

Notice that in both of these passages of Scripture God is complaining about the presentation of the people's worship. In Malachi, He complained that the people put more energy and effort into creating a worthy presentation to impress human governors and dignitaries but they gave a lackluster effort when it came to putting together a presentation for God. God wants our best, too. He doesn't want to be second place in our lives. He doesn't want a Beyonce concert looking the best while His church's worship service looks dull. When our hearts are not into the worship experience and its presentation, that lack of enthusiasm comes across to sinners. They'll begin to wonder why should they be excited about a God that we, God's people, aren't even excited about.

Apparently, God is an extravagant God. The Bible records in 1 Kings chapter six that the temple God instructed King Solomon to build for Him was overlaid with gold; it was built using the finest materials. The Temple of Jerusalem was the most splendid and luxurious structure the world had ever seen. And God didn't stop there. The wealth that God bestowed upon King Solomon was such that it drew attention from every other nation on the face of the earth. Here is a description of Solomon's wealth, which God gave to him, from 2 Chronicles 9:13-28 (God's News Translation):

13 Every year King Solomon received over twenty-five tons of gold,
14 in addition to the taxes paid by the traders and merchants. The kings of Arabia and the governors of the Israelite districts also brought him silver and gold.
15 Solomon made two hundred large shields, each of which was covered with about fifteen pounds of beaten gold,
16 and three hundred smaller shields, each covered with

about eight pounds of beaten gold. He had them all placed in the Hall of the Forest of Lebanon.

17 The king also had a large throne made. Part of it was covered with ivory and the rest of it was covered with pure gold.

18 Six steps led up to the throne, and there was a footstool attached to it, covered with gold. There were arms on each side of the throne, and the figure of a lion stood at each side.

19 Twelve figures of lions were on the steps, one at either end of each step. No throne like this had ever existed in any other kingdom.

20 All of King Solomon's drinking cups were made of gold, and all the utensils in the Hall of the Forest of Lebanon were of pure gold. Silver was not considered valuable in Solomon's day.

21 He had a fleet of ocean-going ships sailing with King Hiram's fleet. Every three years his fleet would return, bringing gold, silver, ivory, apes, and monkeys.

22 King Solomon was richer and wiser than any other king in the world.

23 They all consulted him, to hear the wisdom that God had given him.

24 Each of them brought Solomon gifts—articles of silver and gold, robes, weapons, spices, horses, and mules. This continued year after year.

25 King Solomon also had four thousand stalls for his chariots and horses, and had twelve thousand cavalry horses. Some of them he kept in Jerusalem and the rest he stationed in various other cities.

26 He was supreme ruler of all the kings in the territory from the Euphrates River to Philistia and the Egyptian border.

27 During his reign silver was as common in Jerusalem as stone, and cedar was as plentiful as ordinary sycamore in the foothills of Judah.

28 Solomon imported horses from Musri and from every other country.

To be honest, King Solomon makes Floyd Mayweather look like a junkie. According to financial analysts, King Solomon's net-worth exceeded 20 trillion dollars. That is a true testament to the extravagance of God. God demanded the best of everything: the first and the best flocks, the best materials to build His house. Likewise, God requires the best from us.

God is not a broke God. That is why one of the promises of God to His people is wealth and material prosperity. God desires that we not only show off His power but that we also show off His prosperity so that the world may marvel. Sadly, much of the church has fallen for the lie that God's people are supposed to be broke and busted. But 3 John 1:2 tells us that God desires for us to "prosper" physically even as our souls prosper. God, in 2 Corinthians chapter nine, promises to bless us financially so that we'll always be able to give to those in need and bless His house. Jesus said in Matthew 10:29-30 (NLT), "…and I assure you that everyone who has given up house or brothers or sisters or mother or father or children or property, for my sake and for the Good News, will receive now in return a hundred times as many houses, brothers, sisters, mothers, children, and property—along with persecution. And in the world to come that person will have eternal life." Notice that Jesus said we'll receive material blessings in this life and in the world to come, although persecution will come along with it. I can't find anywhere in the Bible where Jesus promised us poverty as a blessing. I find where He promises not only to meet all of our physical needs but to do "immeasurably more than all we ask or imagine, according to his power that is at work within us" (Ephesians 3:20, NIV).

So, being that God is an extravagant God with expensive tastes who desires to be showered with the finest and most creative offerings during worship and who wants us to endeavor to provide for Him the best, most creative presentation during worship; and not only that, but He also desires to shower us with immeasurable wealth for the purpose of financing His Kingdom activities on the earth, getting the attention of sinners, and blessing our own families so that we can leave an inheritance for our children, grandchildren, and even our great-grandchildren (Proverbs 13:22; Psalm 112:1-3), then we need to ask ourselves, "Why are we content with church as usual?" We should be striving to create a worship experience that makes the Super Bowl halftime look like a night at Joe's Crab Shack. We should showcase the luxury, extravagance, power, glory, and awesomeness of God in front of the world so much so until Millennials bust down our doors wanting to be a part of the worship experience. We should strive to see worship experiences where wheelchairs are lined up against the walls, pushed aside by those that once occupied them; where miracles are commonplace like it was in the church of Acts; where every worship service is an unforgettable experience. Never should we feel as if there are limits to the awesomeness of God. Never should we feel as if God's presence is a flash-in-the-pan that gets old and boring and loses its luster and appeal, one that we easily become desensitized to. No! There are realms of God's glory we've never seen before, realms our flesh can't even handle. God's presence is so euphoric that even the angels in heaven can't get enough. What's our problem?

If we lift God up with all our hearts, minds, and souls, His power will draw the lost, but are we hungry enough for His presence? His presence will transform the sinners and the religious alike, but we must be hungry for His presence. We must remember that the church is not a country club, but the house of the living God. Lift up the gates so that the King of Glory may make His grand entrance week after week. Watch and see if every week His glory doesn't grow more intense.

GET YOUR TOOL BOX

The Bible is a book of tools. Just as there are different baits to use to catch different fish, there are different tools used to clean them. The Bible provides us with the tools needed to deal with different people and different situations. If you want to open a clam, lobster, or a crab, you'll need a set of pliers or a crab opener. Imagine trying to take a tire off of a car using a screwdriver. It wouldn't work. Without the right tool in a situation, all you'll do is exhaust and frustrate yourself. Likewise, you can't use pliers to gut a snapper or bass or white fish; you need a knife for that. It is important that you ask the Holy Spirit to show you the right tool needed to clean the individual, keeping in mind that each person is unique. Even if a person is in the same situation as another, their mentality might be different, their perspective may be different, the way they mentally process what was done to them differs, and this makes that person's situation unique.

Jesus, during the Great Commission, instructed us to "make disciples" of all people in Matthew 28:19. Jesus allowed His disciples to walk with Him for three and a half years. Discipleship is a process that takes time. It doesn't happen overnight. You have to be patient with a person when they're just coming to the faith. Don't expect growth and changes to occur overnight. Think about yourself, when you first got saved. How long did it take for you to grow and mature and break some habits? It took a while. In fact, you're still coming out of some things...and you've been saved for years. So, when it comes to dealing with others, you have to find out what their specific needs are and find out what works for them and patiently work with them. Some people are visual learners, so sitting them down and putting a book in their hands may not help them as much. Some people, you might have to give them the Bible on CD because they receive information better when it's auditory. You need different tools for different situations, which is the reason why there exist multiple ministries within a church. Consider these tools that are often overlooked but are useful in a church: Divorce Ministry, Entrepreneurship Training, Parenting Class, Sex and the Bible Class (designed to help people struggling with sexual identity). You have so many people that have different situations that are just waiting for you to come up with a specific tool (ministry) designed to meet their specific need. With the guidance of the Holy Spirit, you will know what method works best when dealing with each individual God sends your way. God will teach you how to love them, how to break through their defenses and reach their heart, how to best communicate the love of God to them, how to handle them. God has given all of us a tool to help someone else in need, you just have to let the Holy Spirit guide you in this matter.

CHAPTER SIX

KEEPING MILLENNIALS ENGAGED IN THE CHURCH

ILLENNIALS ARE AN INTERESTING GROUP. CHANCES are, if you were to attempt to hold a conversation with Millennials, you'd find it difficult to get, let alone hold on to, their attention. You'd find yourself competing with their cell-phones for their attention. Their faces would probably be buried in their cell-phones as if they're about to be sucked into them. During Sunday morning worship service, you can easily scan the audience and find Millennials with their heads down looking at their cell-phones, reading Facebook posts or Instagram posts or passing text messages back and forth with their friends. This is easily the most distracted generation. The question today is how do we captivate an audience that has so many distractions? How do we become a distraction to the distractions? How do we not just get Millennials into our churches, but also keep them engaged?

Reaching Millennials with the Gospel message is an

uphill battle. There's so much that the church has to compete with for the attention of Millennials. We have to compete with the entertainment industry, with technology, and with the natural tendency to zone-out and lose attention due to short attention-spans. When you think about it, not only is the church in a battle with technology and the entertainment industry for the attention of the youth, but we must compete with academia as well. In schools and universities, many youths are introduced to atheistic and humanistic views that contradict the Christian doctrine. Youths are introduced seven days a week, eight hours a day to the idea that they came from monkeys through the process of evolution, but the Sunday School teacher only gets one hour a week on the weekends to convince them that they're created in the image of God—and that's only if they show up to Sunday School. That's an uphill battle. And then there's the everyday hustle and bustle of life that distracts many Millennials. Many of them are too busy building their careers, chasing after a dollar, and trying to survive the rising cost of living to focus on God.

Let's face it, not even Jesus won everyone over. Jesus was insanely popular, but He didn't reach everyone. He wasn't accepted by everyone. There were some people even He lost. In John 6:48-66, several followers of Christ turned their backs on Him after misinterpreting His words. I'm not going to attempt to claim that I have a magic formula for grabbing and keeping every Millennial in the church. There is no magic formula. But what I can say is there are certain things you can do to increase your chances of drawing and keeping Millennials in your church. I can't promise you that every Millennial will stay in-tune with your sermon—that no Millennial will glance down at their cell-phone during your sermon and check their Facebook while you're preaching your heart out. But what I can tell you is there is a way to grab Millennials' attention and increase the likelihood that they'll choose you over Facebook during the service. Here are a few tips on how to keep Millennials engaged in your church:

TAILOR YOUR SERMONS

Tailor your sermons to address their needs and concerns. This is extremely important. If your sermon isn't addressing the issues that pertain to Millennials, they won't tune-in and listen. In many churches, there is a tendency of pastors to focus on ministering to the Baby-boomer crowd. Many of the sermons are filled with themes and subject matters that only cater to an older audience. If all you talk about in your sermon is struggling to pay bills, you will lose the teenagers and young adults who're focused on surviving high school and college life. If all you talk about is giving birth to something, you'll most likely alienate most of the men in your congregation and then lose them. If all you talk about is social security and retirement, achy joints, arthritis, continually use references to Bengay, continually talk about the good ole' days and the way things "used to be," and spend thirty minutes harping on what you think is "wrong with these young folks today," then you're certainly going to lose Millennials.

As a pastor, I am aware of the fact that I have both Baby-Boomers and Millennials in my church. It is important that I reach both crowds. I can't ignore one group while only focusing on the other. Everyone has needs. Everyone sitting in the pews of your church is there because they have a specific need and want to know what God says about them. I have to be conscious of this while crafting my sermons. I have to watch the language and mind the references I use. I may quote the lyrics of an oldie at one point in the message then spit a lyric from Jay-Z the next in order to grab the attention of both groups. I have to find references that Baby-Boomers can relate to and references that Millennials can relate to. I'll spend a moment addressing the hardship of keeping the light bill paid and then address the hardship of keeping the grades up when your friends are trying to distract you in class. It's important to carefully fill your sermons with references that both Baby-Boomers and Millennials will relate to, which means familiarizing yourself with the issues that matter to each group.

When reaching out to Millennials in your sermons, discover the things that matter to Millennials. Do your research. You can do this several ways: get out and talk to young people, especially the young people in your church. Hold a symposium or a special service or meeting and let the young people talk. Don't assume you know what they're thinking just because you were "once young"; instead, sit with a listening ear and hear them out. Find out what their concerns are. Find out what their issues are. Find out what questions are lingering in their minds that they wish the preacher would address on Sunday mornings or during youth services.

Another thing you can do is research online using keywords. For example, when I looked up the top concerns of Millennials today online, several items popped up consistently. Here are a few of these items:

- *Social Justice/Activism*: Millennials are largely tuned-in to the issue of injustice in their countries. Remember: This is the most accepting generation. They want to stamp out injustice wherever they find it. In neighborhoods all across America, we've seen Millennials marching for the cause of social justice, demanding justice for slain Black men killed unjustly by law enforcement officers, demanding that an end be put to racism and discrimination, demanding that Confederate symbols be removed, demand accountability among government figures, demand justice for the contamination of the water in Flint, Michigan, etc. We've seen Millennials camp out on Wall Street, demanding that income equality is administered—railing against the top 1% income earners. When you mention the current injustices being committed against minorities (Blacks, Hispanics, etc.) and women and children (human sex-trafficking, etc.), and you present a call to action, you'll see Millennials tune-in more. Young people want to be a part of something; they want to be a part of a movement. Reports reveal that Millennials are highly involved in donating to social justice causes. With Millennials, it's not enough to just do business; you have to do business with a purpose. Businesses have made charitable activities a part of their business model because of Millennials. For example, one company that's currently producing and selling custom socks, during their commercial, their key focus is this: "For every pair of socks we sell, we'll donate a pair of socks to the needy." They understand that Millennials want to change the world. Millennials don't want to just sit in the pews; they want to be actively changing the world in some way or another for the better. They have energy. Tell them to just sit still and they will turn their attention elsewhere and direct their energy towards other things.

- *Income Inequality*: Millennials are deeply concerned about the widening gap between the rich and the poor. Poverty is a big concern of theirs. Also, Millennials are generally swamped with student loan debt, so the issue of debt and job opportunities is a major issue of theirs. Addressing the crisis of debt and presenting biblical solutions to dealing with it is a must. With this comes another big topic:

- *Entrepreneurship*: Millennials generally lean towards the entrepreneurial route. They've seen internet billionaires like Mark Zuckerberg and others come up with simple ideas that thrust them into unparalleled success and now they feel ready to conquer the world with a simple idea. With the technology that exists today, Millennials are looking to cash in on the next big idea. Youtube sensations are blowing up every day. Millennials are discovering that they can create their own audiences and create their own success. This is a solution to the rising tide of debt and poverty for many. If you can't find a job, create a job. Ministries that tap into this area are prone to catch the attention of Millennials.

- *Climate Change*: Yes, climate change. Much has been said to stoke the flames of fear and concern in this generation about the state of the earth. Regardless of what you may believe about the subject matter, one thing is certain: it sits heavy in the hearts and minds of many youths today. The movement to "go green" has been big, prompting businesses and entire industries to focus more on becoming environmentally responsible. The thing that concerns Millennials the most is the idea of natural catastrophes coming about due to our mishandling of earth's natural resources, among other things.

Are you engaging Millennials by touching on some of these topics? Are you addressing the social injustices with the Word of God? Are you shedding insight on what's happening in our society with God's Word? Are you compelling Millennials to get involved with your ministry by harnessing their energy rather than suppressing it? You can have a feed-the-hungry campaign and drive and rally Millennials together to pull together resources to provide for needy people and families. You can have a stop-the-violence campaign and have Millennials rally together to attack the issue of crime in your neighborhood. Many ministries invest strongly in outreach and missionary trips, noticing how Millennials are so eager to participate for the purpose of impacting the lives of those less fortunate. Don't just talk about the goodness of God; display it (James 2:14-17).

The Bible doesn't tell us to wait until the people come to our churches; it tells us to "compel them to come" in Luke 14:23. The word *compel* in the Greek means "to necessitate." Are you making the church necessary in the eyes of Millennials? Are you helping Millennials understand the necessity of the church by showing them how Christ is able to help them where they are? If Millennials no longer see the church as necessary, they will view it as obsolete.

Another point to bring out regarding tailoring your sermons to reach Millennials is you must keep in mind that the Millennials generation is the "information generation." This generation doesn't want to simply hear "The Lord will make a way"; they want to you to answer those deep-rooted questions about God and the Bible. They want to see the evidence of the validity of Scripture in light of the scientific theories of today. Can you prove that Creationism is valid as opposed to evolution? Can you prove that the Bible is the authoritative Word of God that hasn't been contaminated and tampered with by men? Millennials want to know "Why?" Why is homosexuality a sin? What does God think about abortion? Why should we tithe? Why? Like we covered in the Introduction of this book, Baby-Boomers tend to follow instructions out of a sense of loyalty without asking questions, but Millennials always want to know why they're doing something before they commit to doing it. The more information you present in your messages, the more likely you're going to gain and hold the attention of Millennials.

The "information generation" spends a lot of time receiving information about various religions and beliefs. Millennials aren't confined to the local church; they have the ability to immerse themselves in other beliefs from the comforts of their cell-phones and laptop computers. Nowadays, many Black Millennials are being introduced to the ideas put forth in Egyptology—they're being told they're gods. Many Millennials in America are turning to Eastern religions such as Buddhism and Hinduism—practicing yoga and transcendental meditation. It's not uncommon today to see a Millennial combine different religious beliefs together. For example, you'll find in many churches the practice of "Christian yoga," which is actually being denounced by staunch Hindu leaders as heresy being that they view yoga as a religion, not an exercise. To them, "Christian yoga" is an oxymoron. But Millennials don't see it that way. They are simply on a hunt for more and more information in the quest to expand their minds. With the influx of all of these new ideas and beliefs into our society, the church has to arm itself with the truth and be able to explain in greater detail what differentiates Christianity from other religions and what makes Jesus different from...let's say, Horus and Osiris, or Krishna, or Buddha. Simply saying Jesus is the Messiah isn't enough for many Millennials. You have to prove the validity of the Bible, prove the existence of Jesus, and show using both biblical and non-biblical sources how Jesus truly is the Messiah...on top of demonstrating the power of God. Why? Because Satan has stepped up his efforts to entrap the minds of the youth. So, if Satan has stepped up his game, we must step up ours. There's an entire branch of theology dedicated to the defense of the Gospel; it's called Apologetics. People like C.S. Lewis and Dr. Ravi Zacharias are well-known Christian apologists who've done an excellent job of making the Gospel relevant to our modern generation.

BE AUTHENTIC

One of the biggest turn-offs for Millennials is being inauthentic, fake, phony. One of the things that will drive Millennials out of your church running and screaming is when the members therein act and pretend as if they don't wrestle with issues, have addictions and vices, wrestle with temptations and desires, and have shortcomings of their own. Millennials esteem honesty and ethics as their top concerns in the workplace; and hence, they expect these things in the church. Honesty is important. Being open and honest is an ingredient in communication. If you sense that a person you're dealing with is being dishonest, you'll undoubtedly end any association with that person. When you're honest, people will trust you. Regarding Millennials, as I mentioned before, one of their biggest issues with the church is trust— they feel as if they can't trust the church. Being transparent and honest about your struggles will establish rapport with others, especially Millennials who already fear that the church is too judgmental. Again, you don't have to stop addressing sin in your sermons, but you have to be transparent and not act as if you don't wrestle with sin like everyone else. Don't become judgmental. Let others know that you're human also, and you need God's grace and mercy also. Be real. Be authentic.

Today, it isn't uncommon to find pastors enjoying things that they couldn't have enjoyed before. For example, you'll find some pastors sitting front row at R&B concerts, whereas, in times past, they wouldn't dare do so. In the past, some preachers were scorned for going to "the picture show" (movies); but today, pastors will post pictures of themselves on Facebook walking into a movie theatre with a bucket of popcorn under their arms. Today, people are becoming more comfortable with being transparent. Furthermore, pastors understand the need to reach people where they are and to relate to them in subtle ways. They understand the importance of not running from the world but running right in the midst of the darkness with the light of the Gospel. In order to do this, you have to be willing to step outside of the walls of the church and associate with those in the dark. You can't isolate yourself among the saints and preach to the choir. Reaching the lost involves going beyond the four walls of the church, and not only that but making yourself approachable. That's what Jesus did. Jesus went to a wedding in Canaan and even turned water into wine so that the party could continue. He didn't sit back and shun the celebration, lifting up his nose at the people as if they were filthy sinners who were too dirty for Him to be around. Jesus placed Himself right in the center of the action, right where all of the sinners were, and He made Himself approachable to them.

The Apostle Paul explains to us that we can't run from the darkness and hide in the light if we're going to evangelize the lost. We have to place ourselves where the action is. Paul wrote in 1 Corinthians 5:9-11 (NLT),

"When I wrote to you before, I told you not to associate with people who indulge in sexual sin. But I wasn't talking about unbelievers who indulge in sexual sin, or are greedy, or cheat people, or worship idols. You would have to leave this world to avoid people like that. I meant that you are not to associate with anyone who claims to be a believer yet indulges in sexual sin, or is greedy, or worships idols, or is abusive, or is a drunkard, or cheats people. Don't even eat with such people."

111

The Apostle Paul explained that you can't hide from people who commit sins—they're everywhere. One of those sinners keeps staring back at you every time you look into the mirror. And if you avoid sinners, who will be there to minister to them. They aren't coming to where you are, so you must go to where they are. But the key thing is to be authentic wherever you go. Learn to enjoy yourself. Be human. Enjoy that action movie. There's nothing wrong with dancing with your spouse. You know how far to go. You know when the music is getting out of hand and it's time to leave the atmosphere. You've been given discernment by the Holy Spirit. But you have to learn how to relax, calm down, stop being so tense as if you don't like being around people, be approachable, enjoy your peace, have fun, let others see that you know how to have fun, and learn to be in the world even though you know this world is not your home.

BE MORE ACCESSIBLE

Take advantage of today's technology. Like I said earlier, if you're not utilizing social media to help build your ministry, you're running behind the curve. You have to go to where the fish are, where the Millennials are. They're on Facebook, Instagram, Twitter, Snapchat, etc. They're on their cell-phones, laptops, and tablets. If you know where they are, then why aren't you going to get them? Place your ministry online. Make sure your church has a website. Make sure your ministry is set up where people can conveniently give online. Make sure your ministry is plugged into social media. You don't have to go live during services, but you do need to make sure you have a strong online presence. Let Millennials see your church in action. Take pictures of your service and post them online. Have the members comment online about how powerful Sunday service was. When there are snow days—days when people can't get out and come to church—take advantage of the live streaming services these social media platforms offer. You may even look into creating an app for your church that Millennials can download to their phones; that way they can instantly stay plugged into the services and contribute financially without any hassle. It's so much easier for a Millennial to simply touch a button and give online using a service like PayPal. It's about convenience. It's about easy accessibility. Millennials move at the speed of light. Today, business moves at the speed of light. People don't like to be patient. Sure, patience is a virtue, but capitalizing on the accessibility and convenience technology brings only puts you in a position to catch the fish more easily.

REFERENCES

INTRODUCTION

1. *40 Percent Of Americans Now 'Prefer Socialism To Capitalism'*. http://www.prophecynewswatch.com/article.cfm?recent_news_id=1554
2. Ehrenfreund, Max. *A majority of millennials now reject capitalism, poll shows.* https://www.washingtonpost.com/news/wonk/wp/2016/04/26/a-majority-of-millennials-now-reject-capitalism-poll-shows/?utm_term=.8123eaa7869a
3. Fleming, John. *Gallup Analysis: Millennials, Marriage and Family.* http://news.gallup.com/poll/191462/gallup-analysis-millennials-marriage-family.aspx

CHAPTER TWO

1. Fingerhut, Hannah. *Millennials' views of news media, religious organizations grow more negative.* http://www.pewresearch.org/fact-tank/2016/01/04/millennials-views-of-news-media-religious-organizations-grow-more-negative/
2. *What Millennials Want When They Visit Church.* https://www.barna.com/research/what-millennials-want-when-they-visit-church/
3. Burroughs, Dillon. *Church, Millennials Don't Trust You.* https://www.jashow.org/articles/guests-and-authors/dillon-burroughs/church-millennials-dont-trust-you/

CHAPTER FOUR

1. Wakefield, Jane. *Social media 'outstrips TV' as news source for young people.* http://www.bbc.com/news/uk-36528256

ABOUT THE AUTHOR

Pastor Jeremy C. Tuck is the Senior Pastor of Living Faith Tabernacle, located in Forest Park, Georgia. He is a man of unbelievable faith and incredible strength. He is a man who knows the word of God and has been preaching it with simplistic truth from the depths of his soul!

Pastor T, as he is affectionately known, is a talented singer, songwriter, and musician who has traveled extensively throughout the United States. His travels have afforded him the opportunity to share the word of God through many venues.

Pastor T holds several degrees, which includes a BA in Biblical Education and Philosophy, a BA in Business Administration, as well as MBA in Business Administration. Through God's grace and his desire for continued education, he is currently pursuing his PhD in Organizational Leadership at Oral Roberts University. He is the face of Men's Health for prostate cancer and has been recently featured in the Better Times Christian Magazine which has been delivered to over 50,000 homes in Atlanta and surrounding areas.

In 2016 Pastor T published and released, "The Let Go Effect". Pastor T serves on the Board of Directors for the Buddy House Children's Sex Trafficking organization, and he is an active member of Habitat for Humanity, and the National Professional Businesses of America.

Pastor T loves spending time with his lovely wife Akila, and their sons, Jeremiah, Ayden, Austin, and Jaxten. Despite having a very busy and involved schedule, he understands that his steps must be ordered by God for there to be any success in his life. He has an unwavering passion for ministry and youth, and strives to reach people where they are, while guiding them to their appointed destiny. His mission through Empowerment, Impact and Influence is to reach and encourage the lost and broken hearted as they seek a place of Refuge. With hopes to lead and guide the Body of Christ to their full potential while embodying spiritual Christianity.

To contact the author, go to

www.lftchurch.com
pastortuck@lftchurch.com
Facebook: @jeremytuck
Instagram: @jeremytuck
Twitter: @jeremytuck